AMISTAD NATIONAL RECREATION AREA: ARCHEOLOGICAL SURVEY AND CULTURAL RESOURCE INVENTORY

By Phil Dering

Submitted to:
National Park Service
Intermountain Cultural Resource Center
P.O. Box 728
Santa Fe, NM   87504-0728

In Partial Fulfillment of
Cooperative Agreement No. 1443-CA-1250-6-005
Between National Park Service and
Texas A&M University

Submitted by:
Center for Ecological Archaeology
Texas A&M University
College Station, Texas 77843-4352

2002

MANAGEMENT SUMMARY

This draft report is submitted in partial fulfillment of Cooperative Agreement No. 1443-CA-1250-6-005 between the National Park Service and Texas A&M University (TAMU). It presents a basic description of the Systemwide Archeological Inventory Survey (SAIP) of 1992 1993, and subsequent surveys conducted during a reservoir drawdown period in 1995, 1996, and 1997. Survey descriptions are based on draft documents and site data recording forms submitted to TAMU.

Following a description of research and resource management objectives, a basic overview of the past and present environment, existing archeological knowledge, and major questions for current and future research are presented. Drawing upon past survey documents and the Archeological Sites Management Information System (ASMIS) database, a summary of survey goals, methods, and a basic description of the cultural resource inventory of the areas surveyed is provided. The report discusses a selected sample of 500 sites, including all sites noted in the SAIP 1992 1993 survey and 102 of the sites noted in the 1995, 1996, and 1997 surveys. Survey areas are estimated from documents, and site density for various sections of the Amistad NRA and adjacent properties is presented.

The sample of 500 sites is discussed and summarized in tabular form. Fourteen prehistoric site types were identified in the database, with 144 sites located wholly or partially on federal property, and the remaining 356 on adjacent private property. The database contains 227 rockshelters, 92 burned rock middens, and 29 caves; these three site types account for 76 percent of all the sites in the project database. In addition to these site types, 25 fire-cracked rock concentrations or scatters, 24 overhangs, 22 lithic scatters, and 16 hearth sites are listed. The database of 500 sites contains a total of 2,477 feature entries 2,380 are prehistoric and 97 are historic. The presence of 109 pictograph features and 183 well-preserved middens in shelters attests to the unusual richness of cultural resources in this region. The discussion summarizes known site attributes, including cultural affiliation, chronology, feature and artifact scatter types, landform category, material culture, and rock art features of the 500 survey sites.

Available survey documents include a scope-of-work providing field approach for the low-water survey, but there is no scope-of work for the SAIP survey. Further, examination of the database provided to Texas A&M University indicates that a single, clearly defined site typology was not applied to all of the surveys. Because site typologies were not consistently applied, efforts are made in the current study to define and apply a single site typology that is consistent with other other regional site designators utilized outside the park. The current report presents a review of previous surveys conducted in the region and provides suggestions for a site typology, field methods, and a minimal site definition. Recommendations for additional research, for field and recording methods, and for future investigations needed to aid future resource management efforts are also discussed.

ACKNOWLEDGMENTS

The investigators are thankful for the cooperation of Robert Powers, Anthropology Division of the National Park Service, Santa Fe. We also thank Joseph Labadie, Park Archeologist at Amistad National Recreation Area for his assistance, and Park Superintendent William Sontag for his support. Steven Baumann, Archeologist and ASMIS Administrator at the Western Archeological and Conservation Center, National Park Service, Tucson, deserves acknowledgment for his assistance with the databases.

Bryan Mason and Michael Crow of the Center for Ecological Archaeology at TAMU were the graphics and GIS managers for the project. Bryan Michael drew many of the maps in AutoCad and compiled the others from ARCView. Student workers and volunteers were Jana Grabbe and David Spatzier. Alston V. Thoms, Center Director, provided advice and administrative support. Many thanks to Robert Powers, Stephen L. Black, Joseph Labadie, and Daniel Potter, for reviewing the report and providing constructive comments.

TABLE OF CONTENTS

LIST OF FIGURES

List of Figures *(Continued)*

LIST OF TABLES

Chapter 1

INTRODUCTION TO THE PROJECT

PROJECT HISTORY AND OBJECTIVES

The purpose of this report is to present results of surveys conducted within the Amistad National Recreation Area (Amistad NRA) under the authority of the Systemwide Archeological Inventory Program initiated by the National Park Service (NPS). Surveys summarized in the current report include the Systemwide Archeological Inventory Program survey of 1992 1993 and the low-water surveys of 1995 1997. An overview of these surveys will assist in providing the Park with the inventory and management information needed to preserve and protect cultural resources under current and future NPS management.

Prior to 1990, the NPS managed natural and cultural resources around Amistad Reservoir for 25 years without a legislative mandate. Passage of Public Law 101-628 provided NPS the mandate to protect and manage the cultural, natural, scenic, recreational, and scientific resources. In addition to the directive to protect and manage cultural resources, the law authorized boundary revisions and provided for acquisition of an additional 1,200 acres of land. In preparation for the acquisition of additional property, NPS was directed to perform a cultural resource survey of land adjacent to Amistad NRA to determine if significant cultural resources existed that should be included in the boundary expansion.

The second impetus to renewed survey efforts in the region came about with the recognition by NPS that most park units in the system lacked reliable and comprehensive information on cultural resources within their boundaries. In response to this need, NPS established an internal archeological survey program, the Systemwide Archeological Inventory Program (SAIP).

The Boundary Expansion Survey (BES) was initiated in December 1991. It was conducted in conjunction with the proposed expansion of land holdings around Amistad NRA, and was specifically organized to gather information about sites scheduled for possible acquisition by the Park (Labadie 1994:20-21). On February 6, 1992, survey of Amistad NRA began under the authority of SAIP, and continued until April 30, 1993. The SAIP was conducted to provide an inventory of archeological sites within Park boundaries. Between 1992-1993, SAIP field efforts were directed by James Mayberry of the NPS Division of Anthropology, Santa Fe. Beginning in 1994, SAIP investigations continued with three surveys designed to document sites newly exposed by falling reservoir levels following periods of severe regional drought. These surveys are referred to as the low-water surveys and were directed by Joseph Labadie, the Amistad NRA Park Archeologist.

Because the SAIP survey followed the BES effort without a break in fieldwork, because many of the BES sites were re-recorded during the SAIP effort, and because many of the field personnel were the same, these two surveys are referred to in the following pages as the BES/SAIP survey, or simply the SAIP survey. Beginning in 1994, additional archeological inventory performed under SAIP standards and guidelines was initiated to document sites exposed by falling reservoir levels following periods of severe drought. These surveys, conducted in 1995, 1996, and 1997, were directed by Joseph Labadie, the Amistad park archeologist. They are referred to herein as the "low-water surveys."

Site data from the SAIP and the low-water surveys have been entered into the Archeological Sites Management Information System (ASMIS). ASMIS serves as the National Park Service's database for basic registration and management of park prehistoric and historic archeological resources. It documents site location, site description, significance, condition, threats, and management requirements for known park archeological sites. The system provides a tool by which site information may be standardized and organized. ASMIS also provides the capability to assemble and report summary data needed for managing archeological resources within a park or group of parks. NPS has integrated the ASMIS into a Geographic Information System (GIS) using ArcView 3.2 GIS software. Basic cultural historical and management information is tied to locational information, and can be accessed using this system. The site distribution maps in this document have been generated using databases prepared by the National Park Service.

The current project has two objectives. First, the report provides a concise, basic description and analysis of surveys conducted from 1991 to 1993 under the auspices of SAIP, and incorporates results of investigations conducted during the low-water surveys from 1995 to 1997. Details of the SAIP 1991 1993 survey have been gleaned from the draft document and associated files (Mayberry 1997), and from site data recording forms. Likewise, background information regarding the low-water surveys was obtained from survey documentation submitted to Texas A&M University. Archeological and management summary data are presented for the 398 sites described during SAIP investigations and for 102 sites described during the low-water surveys. The summary of cultural resources in and adjacent to Amistad NRA is based on the site data in ASMIS and available site data recording forms.

The second objective of this project actually developed during fulfilment of the first objective. It became apparent that differing sets of terms for site types and feature types had been used for the two surveys, resulting in inconsistent data entries into the ASMIS database. Therefore, a primary objective of this project is to provide a research design and a methodological/typological framework around which future archeological surveys can be based in the Amistad NRA.

ORGANIZATION OF THE REPORT

The first part of this report provides research background for the study, including a summary of the regional biophysical environment and cultural history (Chapters 1 and 2). This section also reviews existing gaps in archeological data and discusses the history of archeological surveys conducted in the region. Based upon recognized data gaps and research needs in the region, a research design is presented that includes a review of survey approaches used in the region and a site typology (Chapter 3). Adoption of a consistent site typology and recording methods was needed in order to mold the Amistad NRA survey results into a useable database forma; this is provided in Chapter 4.

The second part of this report summarizes available information on field methods and presents results of the SAIP surveys conducted from 1991 to 1993 and the low-water surveys carried out from 1995 to 1997. Survey data have been incorporated into the ASMIS database using the site typology described in Chapter 5. The resulting ASMIS data are used to present a summary overview of cultural resources within and adjacent to Amistad NRA. The overview includes site types, sizes, components, and temporal associations presented in tabular form. Management information, including site conditions, evaluations, and management recommendations recorded by field crews, are also summarized in tabular form. The progress made by previous surveys is evaluated, and suggestions for future research are presented (Chapter 6). Appendix A reproduces the Task Directive for Archeological Survey, and the survey model for 1995, 1996, and 1997 low-water surveys is reproduced in Appendix B.

Chapter 2

PRESENT AND PAST ENVIRONMENT

Amistad NRA is located in southern Val Verde County on the United States side of the international border, adjacent to the state of Coahuila, Mexico. It includes the canyon areas of the Rio Grande, the Pecos River, and the Devils River, up to the 1,144.3 ft elevation contour, for a total of 57,292 acres (Figure 2.1). The center of Amistad Reservoir lies approximately at 32°30' North latitude and 101°5' West longitude. Because the reservoir is situated at or near the areal limits of several distinct physiographic, biological, and climatic regions, it might be supposed that this ecotonal location had significant effects on Holocene period human activities withing the limits of the park boundaries. As discussed in the following pages, ecotonal differences are spread across a very broad geographic area, and seem likely to have had the greatest impacts on behavior over areas that extend beyond the boundaries of the park. The first part of this chapter provides the environmental context within which to place the archeological surveys.

The second part of this chapter establishes a cultural-historical context for the Amistad NRA. It discusses current subsistence and settlement models that have been proposed for the region, and provides a synthesis of existing data related to a land use-oriented research design.

PHYSICAL ENVIRONMENT

Physiography and Topography

The study area lies at the southwestern edge of the Edwards Plateau division of the Great Plains Physiographic province (Fenneman 1931). It is located in the middle Rio Grande basin (Arbingast et al. 1976; Direccion General De Geografia 1980) where the river flows in a southeasterly direction toward the Gulf of Mexico. The middle and lower Rio Grande is fed by only three major streams along its length, Rio Conchos, the Pecos River, and the Devils River. The Pecos River runs through the western section of the study region, and the Devils River flows through the eastern part of the region.

North of the Rio Grande, topography is level to hilly and is deeply dissected by numerous canyons. Within the immediate boundaries of Amistad NRA, elevation above sea level varies from a low of 940 ft (290 m) at the confluence of the Devils River and the Rio Grande, to a high of 1,300 ft (400 m) along the canyon rim of the Pecos River in the western reaches of the park.

The Lower Pecos cultural region, as defined by Turpin (1995), contains much greater diversity than the landscape located within the Amistad NRA. The Rio Grande embankment is dissected by increasingly precipitous canyons and arroyos which trend north-south toward the Rio Grande. The southern edge of the Edwards Plateau meets the Rio Grande 10 km west and north of Del Rio, Texas, on the United States' side of the river (Fenneman 1931:51). South of the Rio Grande, a plain is dissected by north-trending intermittent streams that originate in the Serranias de los Burros, a mountain range rising to almost 5,000 ft (1,524 m) within 100 km of the Rio Grande. These mountains parallel the Sierra del Carmen of Mexico and the southern escarpment of the Edwards/Stockton Plateau, trending northeast-southwest from the Rio Grande to the Planos del Coahuila. The southern part of the Burros are dominated by the 4,700-ft-tall Cerro Oso Blanco, which is located about 70 km (43 mi) southwest of Del Rio. The largest streams draining the Burros are the Arroyo de la Zorra, which enters the Rio Grande near the midpoint of Amistad Reservoir, and the Rio San Diego, a permanent stream which enters the Rio Grande about 60 km downstream from Amistad Dam (Smith 1970).

The deep canyons and limestone topography of the region give rise to numerous permanent or temporary streams and springs that stand in contrast to the xeric nature of the plains and plateau country that they dissect. Amistad Reservoir is fed by three permanent streams – the Rio Grande, the Pecos River, and the Devils River. The Pecos River enters the Rio Grande just 26 mi (42 km) northwest of the confluence of the Rio Grande and the Devils River. On the eastern side of the reservoir, numerous intermittent streams, such as Rough Canyon and San Pedro Creek, enter the Devils River.

Due to its location at the southwestern edge of the Edwards Plateau, many large springs are located within and adjacent to the study area. The southern edge of the Edwards Plateau is delimited by the Balcones Escarpment or fault zone. Some of the largest springs in Texas are located along this fault zone. Faulting along the edge of the plateau has brought the Edwards Aquifer into contact with impervious chalks and marls which, in turn, forces the water to escape to the surface under artesian pressure (Brune 1981:15). San Felipe Springs are the fourth largest springs in Texas and still serve as the sole source of water for the city of Del Rio. Goodenough Springs, also one of the largest springs in Texas, is located beneath the waters of Amistad Reservoir in a side canyon of the Rio Grande (Brune 1981). Although surface water was confined to narrow canyons, numerous springs also existed on the plains to the south of the Rio Grande. Precipitation and water availability definitely affected biomass and local land use, but the abundance of permanent streams and springs indicates that water was seldom a limiting factor to regional mobility (Dering 1999). The inhabitants of, or travelers through, the study area would have easily found water on the landscape north of the Rio Grande and on forays to the Edwards Plateau, to the Lower Pecos region, or across the Rio Grande Plains for a radius of least 100 km (62 mi). Travel to the Burro Mountains along the major arroyos likewise would not have been impeded by a lack of water.

Geology and Soils

Outcrops of Boquillas and Eagle Ford (Upper Cretaceous) and Salmon Peak (lower Cretaceous) limestone prevail throughout the study area. To the northeast, the south-facing scarp of the Edwards Plateau is dominated by outcrops of upper Cretaceous and lower Cretaceous limestones. Gravels of Miocene-Pliocene age, commonly called Uvalde Gravels, are present particularly around San Pedro Creek. Uvalde Gravels are an important geological surface feature; their distribution corresponds with the location of several prehistoric lithic quarry sites within the Amistad NRA near San Pedro Canyon. Uvalde Gravels were first labeled and described by Hill (1891:368) to refer to upland gravel deposits in South Texas, and they are mapped as a distinct geological unit distinguishable from the Quaternary High Gravels of Central Texas. From the Del Rio Sheet, Geologic Atlas of Texas (Barnes 1977), Uvalde Gravels are mapped as a Tertiary or Quaternary unit overlying area Cretaceous rocks. They extend over a large portion of southwestern Kinney County, northwestern Maverick County, and the southern portion of Val Verde County (Barnes 1977).

Soils are dominated by the Langtry-rock-outcrop complex, a shallow, rocky soil with 45-70 percent exposed bedrock. In the flats, Val Verde silty clay loam is most common. In the eastern section of the study area around San Pedro Creek and Rough Canyon, soils are composed of the Olmos gravelly loam, Val Verde silty clay loam, Amistad flaggy clay loam, and Acuña silty clay (Golden et al. 1982).

MODERN CLIMATE

The immediate study area has an average annual rainfall of 44 cm (17.2 in) (Office of the State Climatologist 1987). Most precipitation occurs in two peaks, one in spring (April-May) and one in early fall (September-October). This bimodal pattern is consistent with most of Texas except the Trans-Pecos/Big Bend region, which has a summer monsoonal precipitation peak (Schmidt 1995). The driest months of the year in the project area occur in winter from November to March, and in summer from June to August (Golden et al. 1982; Office of the State Climatologist 1987).

The frost-free period averages 300 days between February 13 and December 8. The average annual temperature is 70°F, ranging from a low of 51°F in January to a high of 86°F in July (Golden et al. 1982). Most precipitation during both rainy peaks results from thunderstorms at frontal boundaries fed by moisture from the Gulf of Mexico (Norwine 1995).

Although these averages communicate a general impression of climate, the truly interesting aspect of southern Texas climate is its variability. The Amistad region is positioned at two great climatic crossroads of the continent — the sharp dividing line between the humid east and the arid west, and the more ambiguous division between the seasonal mid-latitude regimes to the north and the winterless tropical climes to the south (Norwine 1995:140). As a result, the region encompassing southern Texas and northeastern Mexico has a semiarid, subtropical climate with dry winters and hot summers (Golden et al. 1982:2; Norwine 1995:138). The region is marked by moisture-deficient, semidesert precipitation regimes with greater mean coefficients of interannual rainfall variability than any other semiarid region in the world, except northeastern Brazil (North et al. 1995:47; Norwine 1995:140). In other words, the region has high interannual variability in precipitation, making longer trends in precipitation extremely difficult to predict. It is considered a marginal region for intensive land use — an area where plant and animal populations are quickly affected by fluctuations in precipitation.

Drought frequently and unpredictably occurs in the region, as reflected by high interannual variability in precipitation (Norwine 1995:140). Areas within and adjacent to the Trans-Pecos region often undergo periods of prolonged, below-average rainfall. This is especially true for winter droughts due to the intrusion of cold, dry, polar air into the region. Throughout the Holocene, it is likely that climatic boundaries of the Chihuahuan Desert continually expanded and contracted in response to the long-term migration and strength of the large, subtropical ridge of high pressure that for much of the year, surrounds the earth above the equator (Schmidt 1986). The size and strength of this subtropical ridge depends upon the occurrence of El Niño, volcanic eruptions, and variability of the coupled atmospheric-ocean system (North et al. 1995).

BIOLOGICAL ENVIRONMENT

The study area lies within a major transition zone at a point where three great biotic provinces and their characteristic vegetation areas converge (Figure 2.2). It is actually positioned at the junction of the Tamaulipan, Balconian and Chihuahuan Biotic provinces (Blair 1950:98).

Vegetation

Given the area's ecotonal status, its flora and fauna exhibit elements of all three provinces. Amistad Reservoir is located at the western edge of the South Texas Plains vegetation area in the Tamaulipan Lower Pecos province (Blair 1950:98; Hatch et al. 1990:2). Vegetation grades into

Chihuahuan Desert Scrub, which occupies the lower canyonlands of the Devils River, the Pecos River, and the Rio Grande (Brown 1982:171). About 20 km north of the study area, vegetation grades into the juniper-oak savannah associated with the Edwards Plateau (Amos and Gehlbach 1988; Hatch et al. 1990:2).

Vegetation in the region is a savannah, which is a tension zone between woody and herbaceous plants. Depending on local or regional environmental or anthropic conditions, the area may favor shrubs or grasslands (Archer 1990; Archer et al. 1988). Amistad Reservoir is located at the western edge of the mesquite-blackbrush acacia savannah of southern Texas, in the Tamaulipan Lower Pecos province (Blair 1950:98; Hatch et al. 1990:2). To the west, vegetation rapidly grades into sotol-lechuguilla-creosote bush vegetation which occupies the lower canyonlands of the Devils River, the Pecos River, and the Rio Grande, commonly associated with the Chihuahuan Desert (Brown 1982:171).

Despite the fact that the region is technically a savannah, woody plants dominate the vegetation in most upland areas within the boundaries of the reservoir today. These include mesquite (*Prosopis glandulosa*), several species of acacia (*Acacia* spp.), whitebrush (*Aloysia gratissima*), Texas persimmon (*Diospyros texana*), blue sage (*Salvia ballotiflora*), lotebush (*Ziziphus obtusifolia*), various buckthorns (*Condalia* spp.), and spiny hackberry (*Celtis pallida*). Creosote (*Larrea tridentata*) and ceniza (*Leucophyllum frutescens*) are prominent in many areas. Along the upper reaches of canyons, succulents and rosette-stemmed evergreens are also common, including prickly pear and tasajillo (*Opuntia* spp.), several yuccas (*Yucca* spp.), and *Agave lechuguilla*. Small trees are confined to narrow canyons or creek terraces. Littleleaf walnut (*Juglans microcarpa*), several species of oak (*Quercus* spp.), Mexican ash (*Fraxinus greggi*), and Texas persimmon (*Diospyros texana*) are a few of the more prominent tree resources located in the canyons. A large stand of Huisache (*Acacia farnesiana*) and mesquite (*Prosopis glandulosa*) is located on terraces associated with San Pedro Creek.

Vertebrate Fauna

Very little research has been completed regarding vertebrate fauna of the region. The only extensive records of vertebrate fauna around the study area are derived from inventories of the Amistad Reservoir, where 60 species of mammalian vertebrates have been noted (Ditton and Schmidly 1977:82). During a brief reconnaissance of the Amistad Reservoir area, Raun (1966) identified 52 species of amphibians and reptiles.

Vertebrate remains have been recovered from Hinds Cave in the Lower Pecos region, where Lord (1984) identified 60 vertebrate taxa, including deer, antelope, rabbits, birds, lizards, snakes, and fish. As Saunders (1986) noted, although the inhabitants practiced a broad-spectrum type of economy, small game supplemented by deer provided most of the meat. The faunal record from Hinds Cave indicates that during the time period from the Early Archaic through the Late Archaic (9000-1200 B.P.), the species composition of vertebrate fauna did not noticeably change (Lord 1984).

Summary

Although Amistad NRA exhibits biological diversity resulting from its location at the junction of three main Lower Pecos provinces, it does not provide an abundance of any single plant or animal resource. Diversity does not equate with high biomass or an abundance of resources. For this reason it is quite likely that the hunter-gatherers of the region maintained a high degree of residential mobility (Dering 1999; Sobolik 1996). Further, a dissected plateau has much less relief than the Basin and Range Province which lies to the west and southwest of the study area. For example, in the Chisos Mountains of Big Bend, one may climb from a lechuguilla-creosote bush flat to a woodland dominated by piñon and Douglas fir in less than a day. During a walk of similar distance in the Amistad NRA, no such change occurs. The traveler passes through several canyons and uplands with corresponding microenvironmental changes, but remains in essentially the same mix of plant and animal species. Major changes in species composition and biomass gradually occur from east to west across the study area, but the full impact of the change is not realized until one passes beyond the limits of the park. Generally speaking, both rainfall and biomass decrease from east to west. Nevertheless, Amistad NRA is located at the junction of these biotic zones, and populations moved through and beyond the immediate study area during the Holocene. Cultural ties have been noted between the Lower Pecos area and the Edwards Plateau to the north and east, to the Burro Mountains to the southwest, and to the South Texas Plains to the southeast. These links will be summarized in Chapter 3.

PALEOENVIRONMENT OF THE LOWER PECOS

Despite the remarkable detail of the prehistoric vegetation record contained in numerous, well-preserved rockshelter deposits, knowledge of the Lower Pecos River paleoenvironmental history is limited to general trends that occurred through the millennia. Pollen and macroplant remains are poorly preserved at the few well-stratified, open, alluvial terrace sites which have been studied in the region (Figure 2.3). Although many Lower Pecos rockshelters have much better plant preservation than open sites, they present a poor environmental record because occupational and post-occupational disturbance mixes strata and artificially introduces quantities of pollen-bearing plant materials that skew the pollen diagram and obscure the image of regional vegetation. The plant vegetation record in rockshelters can also be skewed by cultural selection (Dering 1979).

Distribution of Chihuahuan Desert plants expanded and contracted throughout the late Pleistocene and Holocene periods, leaving widespread relict populations in favorable microenvironments that were primarily influenced by local availability of effective moisture. This resulted in pockets of vegetation refugia unevenly distributed across broad geographic areas. Canyons are one of the most prominent refugia in the region (Van Devender 1990). Because all rockshelters and alluvial terraces are located within canyons, all prehistoric vegetation records from the Lower Pecos River region originate from localities of inherent vegetation stability that would tend to mask all but the most drastic vegetation changes.

Pollen rain has the potential to record regional rather than local vegetation changes. Bryant and Holloway (1985) interpreted falling frequencies of pine pollen as indications that the region was slowly drying throughout the Holocene, with a brief mesic interval occurring around 2,500 years ago marked by an increase in pine and grass pollen frequencies. Bison bone was present at Bonfire Shelter (Val Verde County) and Arenosa Shelter (Val Verde County) until 10,000 B.P. After 10,000 B.P., a general drying trend has been interpreted from gradually falling pine pollen frequencies, and from the absence of bison in the region (Bryant 1969; Dering 1979). The mesic period identified by increased pine and grass pollen around 2500 B.P. is also marked by the return of bison to the region, as indicated in deposits from Arenosa and Bonfire shelters (Bryant 1969).

Throughout the Holocene, pine pollen most likely arrived in the Lower Pecos region via long-distance transport from the Serranias de los Burros, 85 km to the west-southwest. Another source is from several stands of piñon on or near the southern scarp of the Edwards Plateau 98 km to the east in Val Verde County, although no pine wood fragments or pine nuts have been identified from deposits in Lower Pecos River rockshelters (Dering 1979).

While pollen provides a very general view of regional vegetation, most of what is known about the species composition of local vegetation has been gleaned from macroplant analysis of archeological deposits recovered from dry caves in the Lower Pecos River region. Macrobotanical remains give an in depth view of locally available plant resources. This view is admittedly skewed by human selection, but over 120 plant taxa have been identified from Hinds Cave (Dering 1979), a much more comprehensive floral list than is available from any open site.

The best archeobotanical records from rockshelters include the pollen record from Bonfire Shelter (Bryant 1969) and the marcobotanical records from Hinds Cave (Dering 1979; Shafer and Bryant 1977) and Baker Cave (Hester 1983: Sobolik 1991). Macroplant assemblages from Hinds Cave indicate that plants common in the Lower Pecos today, including lechuguilla (*Agave lechuguilla*), yuccas (*Yucca torreyi* and *Y. rostrata*), sotol (*Dasylirion texanum*), acacias (*Acacia greggii* and *A. rigidula*), prickly pear (*Opuntia phaeacantha*), shin oak (*Quercus pungens* var. *vaseyana*), mesquite (*Prosopis glandulosa*,) and juniper (*Juniperus* spp.), were present in the Lower Pecos River region by 9000 B.P. (Dering 1979, 1999).

At Baker Cave on the more mesic Devils River, matrix contents of a hearth dated to 9550 B.P. contained fruits and nuts of trees and shrubs associated with riparian and canyon rim vegetation. However, there was no documentation of lechuguilla, a plant associated with the Chihuahuan Desert, or sotol, a plant associated with both the Chihuahuan Desert and the western and southern Edwards Plateau (Hester 1983:111). Sotol first appears in Baker Cave deposits within a poorly preserved fiber lens dated around 6500 B.P. (Brown 1991:122, Figure 4.17). Other fiber that may represent either sotol or lechuguilla is present in these lower lenses, but it is not clearly identifiable. Brown believes that the absence of sotol and lechuguilla in the earlier deposits may more likely be the result of the very poor preservation environment within certain lower levels of Baker Cave than from any major environmental changes (Ken Brown, personal communication 1996). Riverine canyon vegetation, including littleleaf walnut, Mexican persimmon, netleaf hackberry, grape, and sycamore, were also present at Hinds Cave (Dering 1979) and Baker Cave (Hester 1983).

The Hinds Cave macrobotanical record reveals that by 9000 B.P., the major woody and evergreen-rosette plants that characterize regional vegetation were in place. After that, two notable occurrences mark the mid Holocene. First, the beginning of bulk processing of lechuguilla is indicated by the presence of a large earth oven, accurately dated to 6100 B.P. Brown (1991) has termed the presence of earth ovens in rockshelters as the beginning of an economy of scale, an indication of either population pressure, environmental pressure, or both. Second, juniper wood charcoal, very common in earlier shelter deposits, disappears after 5000 B.P. Juniper apparently grew in the uplands on slightly deeper soils near stands of lechuguilla in the Lower Pecos canyonlands until that time. Today, although isolated junipers grow in sheltered canyons throughout the region, juniper is most common on the uplands above 540 m elevation and 15 km to the north of Hinds Cave (Dering 1979).

A detailed pollen record from Diamond Y Cienega, a middle-elevation desert wetland located in northern Pecos County, recorded a mesic shortgrass prairie between 7000 and 6000 B.P. Around 5000 B.P., the vegetation changed to a shrubland most likely dominated by saltbush. This has been interpreted as a shift to more arid conditions (Hoyt 2000), and roughly corresponds with the disappearance of juniper wood charcoal from the Hinds Cave assemblage.

Around 2500 B.P., one brief return to higher effective moisture is indicated by an increase in grass and arboreal pollen in the Bonfire Shelter record (Bryant 1969; Bryant and Holloway 1985). By 2000 B.P., the pollen records of the Lower Pecos suggest a return to drier conditions and a gradual increase in aridity to the present day (Bryant and Holloway 1985). The Diamond Y Cienega pollen record noted a shift around 3000 B.P. from desert shrubland to a grassland dominated by xeric short grasses, which is interpreted as a slightly more mesic precipitation pattern (Hoyt 2000).

Despite the lack of change in species composition in the rockshelter assemblages of the Lower Pecos, the manner in which the vegetation was distributed across the landscape probably changed often during the last 8,000 years. The region is known to be a savannah/grassland, an area of tension between woody and herbaceous plants; therefore, the physiognomic expression changed as the availability of effective moisture increased or decreased.

Other evidence of climatic change is considered too weak to be accepted without corroborating data from other sources. Geomorphic data from the Lower Pecos River, gleaned from alluvial deposits at the mouths of the Pecos and Devils Rivers, indicate alternating sequences of frequent, gentle overbank flooding, followed by irregular, catastrophic floods (Patton and Dibble 1982). Catastrophic, irregular floods, recorded between 4700 and 3700 B.P., are interpreted as indications of dry periods. The episodes of gentle overbank flooding that occurred around 9500 B.P. and between 3700 and 2700 B.P. have been interpreted as relatively mesic periods of comparatively reliable rainfall (Patton and Dibble 1982). Although the stratigraphic sequence is fairly well dated with 16 radiocarbon assays, Patton and Dibble's work is primarily a flood study, and little attention was paid to identification and characterization of paleosols.

Radiocarbon ages have been obtained from whewellite, a calcium-oxalate-based mineral produced by the lichen *Aspicilia calcarea* that grows on canyon and rockshelter walls in the region (Russ et al. 1996). The whewellite crust forms during extended dry periods and hence is a marker for hot periods with less effective moisture. First, the dates cluster into four xeric episodes – 6000 to 6400 B.P., 2800 to 5000 B.P., 1760 to 2100 B.P., and 680 to 1360 B.P. Second, these xeric episodes appear to correspond in part to the climatic sequence presented by Bryant (1969). This is an unverified but potentially useful source of proxy data for climatic interpretation.

Paleoenvironment: Discussion and Conclusions

Several key concepts can be determined from this review of the environment. First, understanding the geographic context of the study area is critical to constructing an accurate land-use model. Vegetation is a semiarid savannah characterized by tension zones between woody plants and grasslands. The second point is that generally speaking, the regional biomass increases as one moves from west to east within the study area. This is mainly due to the availability of larger deer populations along the well-watered streams and prairie margins to the east of Amistad NRA. The third point is that the study area lies in a dissected plateau. Unlike the Chihuahuan Desert to the west that is marked by basin-and-range topography, there is little elevation change and accordingly little ecological diversity to accompany it. The biodiversity seen within the region is manifested as a gradual change across a broad geographic area. It is most pronounced along an east-west transect, from the Devils River to the area beyond the Pecos River, and is primarily due to geographic variation in average annual rainfall. As a result, any human response to unfavorable downturns in local environmental conditions would have required extreme mobility since the entire area constitutes essentially the same biological zone or habitat.

A final point, and perhaps the most important point to consider, is that the study area lies within a region of uncertain climate. It is located on the border between moist eastern and arid western North America, and between the middle seasonal latitudes and the frost-free tropics. Interannual variability of precipitation is extremely high. This extreme short-term variability may have an averaging effect in the available proxy climatic records. That is, vegetation adapted to both short-term and long-term drought, the very conditions that most likely persisted throughout the Holocene. The repeated short-term drought cycles would favor arid-adapted vegetation and would tend to mask the vegetation expression of the Hypsithermal, a long-term drought cycle. This may explain why regional paleoclimatic records appear relatively stable and why temporal variation in the regional plant assemblages from several sites is very slight.

Chapter 3

ARCHEOLOGY OF THE LOWER PECOS REGION

The archeology of the region provides one of the best preserved and longest records of hunter-gatherer lifeways in North America. The Lower Pecos, with its remarkable concentration of midden deposits in rockshelters and polychrome rock paintings provides unique opportunities to investigate foraging adaptations in a semiarid environment. Since subsistence patterns of hunter-gatherer groups are closely tied to the land on which they make a living, one would expect that the cultural remains clearly reflect the nature of the environment to which they were adapted. For example, most of the debris recovered from burned rock middens is associated with the construction of earth ovens utilized to cook agave, sotol, yucca, and other root foods (Black et al. 1997). The images painted on the canyon and cave walls reflect a belief system very closely tied to plants and animals observed in the regional environment (Boyd and Dering 1996; Turpin 1995), The following section illustrates the close link between sites and landscape, and places the archeological sites into preliminary cultural, geographic, and environmental contexts.

The following discussion is not a comprehensive review of archaeological research, but instead focuses on the history of archeological survey in the region. Comprehensive reviews of the lower Pecos River region are available in Bement (1989), Labadie (1994) and Turpin (1995). The chapter begins with a brief history of previous research, and then provides an overview of regional archeology, including site types, cultural chronology, subsistence/settlement models. The chapter finishes with a review of surveys undertaken in the region, focusing on field protocol and the results generated by the different approaches that have been used by investigators. The discussion of survey method prepares the ground for the research design presented in Chapter 4.

PREVIOUS ARCHEOLOGICAL RESEARCH IN THE LOWER PECOS

Archeological research began in the early 1930's with the advent of museum sponsored excavations. The Smithsonian Institution, the Witte Museum, and the University of Texas at Austin were involved with these early excavations. The most extensive investigations included work at Fate Bell Shelter (Pearce and Jackson 1933; Thomas 1933) and at Shumla Caves (Martin 1933). Setzler (1934) conducted excavations at Goat and Moorehead Caves for the Smithsonian Institution. During this time Forrest Kirkland and A.T. Jackson began copying and studying the remarkable rock paintings of the region (Jackson 1938; Kirkland and Newcomb 1967). Based on the materials recovered from these excavations, Kelley et al. (1940) labeled the area the Pecos River focus and compiled a trait list.

The next great push in research was provided by the construction of Amistad Reservoir at the confluence of the Pecos and Devils Rivers. The National Park Service established the Archeological Salvage Program field office, which was later placed under the control of the University of Texas and renamed the Texas Archeological Salvage Project. Survey, testing, and several large scale excavation projects were conducted as a result of the Amistad Reservoir project (Collins 1969; Dibble and Prewitt 1967). Although site types in the area include rockshelters, alluvial terraces, burned rock middens, quarries, hearth fields, and burials from several upland and lowland landforms, excavation centered on rockshelters and two alluvial terrace sites. Excavations at rockshelters included Centipede and Damp

Caves (Epstein 1960), Bonfire Shelter (Dibble 1965; Dibble and Lorrain 1968), Parida Cave and Conejo Shelter (Alexander 1970, 1974), and other sites (Nunley et al. 1965; Prewitt 1966). Two deeply stratified sites located on river terraces were also investigated, Arenosa Shelter (Dibble 1967) near the confluence of the Pecos River and the Rio Grande, and the Devils Mouth Site (Johnson 1964) at the confluence of the Devils River and the Rio Grande. After the completion of Amistad Reservoir and related salvage projects, extensive excavations were conducted at Hinds Cave and Baker Cave, two rockshelters with long cultural sequences and dry deposits rich in perishable material remains (Chadderdon 1983; Shafer and Bryant 1977).

The acquisition of Fate Bell Shelter and surrounding properties led to the establishment of Seminole Canyon State Historical Park. Subsequent archeological research in the park included the excavation of Seminole Sink, a burial site, and a survey of archeological resources within the park (Turpin 1982, 1986, 1988). The work associated with Seminole Sink and Baker Cave constitute the only large-scale excavations that were conducted in the lower Pecos River region proper during the 1980s.

However, research into the rock paintings of the region has been fairly active throughout the 1980's and 1990's. Turpin (1984, 1990; 1994) was the first archaeologist to examine the role of rock art in the foraging societies of the region. She refined the definitions of the rock art styles, and began to tie the images depicted in the paintings both to ritual and subsistence activities. Boyd (1992, 1998a and b) continued to refine methods in the study of rock paintings, and devised an interdisciplinary approach to rock art research and interpretation. She also maintains that many of the rock paintings constitute preplanned panels, the product of an individual artisan (Boyd 1998b).

Although it has been recognized that incomplete survey of the areas away from the canyons and rockshelters constituted a major deficiency in the archaeological data base (Bement 1989: 74; Saunders 1986), most attempts to remedy the problem have been limited to upland areas immediately adjacent to Amistad Reservoir. A detailed history of survey method follows the discussion of regional site types and cultural chronology.

SITE TYPES, CULTURAL CHRONOLOGY, AND PALEOECONOMY

Site Types

A review of previous site typologies used for the region reveals the remarkable archeological record within and adjacent to Amistad NRA. Previous research in the region has utilized several different site typologies, and with the exception of Turpin (1982) and Turpin and Davis (1993), no two typologies are the same. A brief review is provided here with the dual objective of introducing the reader to the richness of the regional archeological record, and to establishing a typology which will be utilized at least within the Park. A site typology would enable future researchers to obtain results that can be easily reproduced during successive efforts and would eliminate the necessity of going through this process for every new project.

The typologies presented below (Table 3.1) have appeared either in survey reports (Anderson 1974; Graham and Davis 1958; Saunders 1992) or in regional syntheses (Bement 1989; Shafer 1986). The site types fall into two general categories, sheltered and open. For example, rockshelters and caves are cavities located in the walls of the region's deep canyons. These geological phenomena provided protected habitation sites for inhabitants throughout the Holocene. Many rockshelters contain burials, lithic materials, ground stone, desiccated plant remains including sandals and basketry, bones, animal products such as furs or skins, fire-cracked rock (FCR), ash, charcoal, coprolites, and other organic remains in deposits that measure up to 3 m in depth. Sinkholes are solution cavities with openings to the ground surface that often contain burials. Open sites include burned rock middens, rock alignments, ceramic scatters, and alluvial terrace sites. Although most open sites beyond the canyons are comparatively shallow surface manifestations, many stratified sites are located on alluvial terraces at the confluence of major streams, or at the confluence of side canyons and major streams. Most of the sites located on alluvial terraces were inundated by construction of Amistad Reservoir, but several shallower, open sites remain on either alluvial or colluvial terraces inside canyons, and a few remain just downstream from Amistad Dam.

Table 3.1. Prehistoric site types reported by previous surveys in the lower Pecos River region

Graham and Davis (1958)	Anderson (1974)	Turpin (1982)	Shafer (1986)	Bement (1989)	Saunders (1992)	Labadie (1994)
Large rockshelter	Rockshelter	Rockshelter	Rockshelter	Rockshelter	Rockshelter	*Occupational Sites:*
Intermediate rockshelters	Shelter with midden deposit	Rockshelter with art	Cave	Terrace site	Rock art -- petroglyph/ pictograph	Lithic scatter Quarry
Small rockshelter	Open surface site	Burned rock	Alluvial terrace	Lithic procurement/ Quarry	Burned rock midden (>2 m diameter)	Burned rock scatter
Open surface site	Open midden	Stone alignment	Open site	Stone Alignment	Burned rock feature (<2 m diameter)	Burned rock midden Midden Perishable deposit
Buried terrace site	Open burned rock midden	Artifact scatter	Burned rock midden	Hearth field/ ring midden/ large burned rock midden		Bison jump/drive
Stratified terrace site	Buried midden	Lithic scatter	Mortar hole (bedrock feature)	Kill site	Burned rock scatter	*Ceremonial Sites:*
	Overhang	Ceramic scatter	Rock circle (rock alignments)	Burial site	Hearth	Pictograph Petroglyph Burial
	Overhang with midden deposit	Quarry	Burial site	Rock art	Quarry	
	Stone circle		Rock art (Pictograph & petroglyph)		Isolate (<5 artifacts within 5 m)	
	Scattered lithic debris					

Other open sites include lithic procurement and quarry sites that occur on bands of surface gravels that extend into the region from southern Texas. Also, tabular to nodular outcroppings of chert beds are present within exposed areas of limestone bedrock. Hearth fields, ring middens, and burned rock middens comprise a group of site types that are comprised primarily of heat-altered rock and may be located on alluvial or colluvial terraces, or on shallow rocky soils in upland settings. Large areas covered by multiple hearths measuring 1 2 m in diameter are often located on gently sloping colluvial surfaces overlooking drainages, and on upland slopes near canyon headers. Several of these hearth fields have been located since the Amistad Reservoir drawdown in 1994.

A single special-activity, bison-drive site, Bonfire Shelter, has been identified in the region. The site of at least three episodes of bison drives, Bonfire Shelter is composed of large bone beds or strata located at the base of a precipitous cliff in Eagles Nest Canyon (Bement 1989; Turpin 1995).

The rock paintings of the Lower Pecos region constitute perhaps the most spectacular and notable features of Lower Pecos archeology. Although petroglyphs have been reported from the region, no research has been conducted on them. The polychrome and monochrome paintings, on the other hand, have been the subject of numerous studies and have been categorized into four distinctive and temporally successive styles. In order from oldest to youngest, these are: (1) Pecos River; (2) Red Linear; (3) Red

Monochrome; and (4) Historic (Kirkland and Newcomb 1967). Turpin (1995:551) has recently proposed a fifth, intrusive style, the Bold Line Geometric. Recent advances in extracting organic binders from the rock art paints have allowed researchers to obtain radiocarbon assays from the art using accelerator mass spectrometry (AMS).

Each rock art style has specific characteristics and is associated with a different time period (Boyd 1998b; Turpin 1995). The central motif of the Pecos River Style is composed of polychrome and monochrome anthropomorphic figures in association with enigmatic designs. Over twenty AMS dates place the Pecos River Style in the Middle Archaic period, between approximately 4100 and 3000 B.P. (Hyman and Rowe 1997). The Red Linear Style is characterized by small red stick figures of humans and animals associated in groups. This style dates to the Transitional Archaic/Late Prehistoric around 1280 B.P. (Ilger et al. 1994). The Red Monochrome Style consists of front-facing human figures with bows and arrows and animals in side view. Turtles, fish, turkeys, and mammals have been noted in Red Monochrome panels. The radiocarbon assays from the Late Prehistoric place it temporally just a little younger than Red Linear, around 1125 B.P., but the presence of bows and arrows in the paintings place it in the Late Prehistoric (Ilger et al. 1995). Many motifs in the pictographs have been associated with shamanic ritual (Boyd 1998b; Turpin 1990, 1994).

Turpin (1986, 1995:551) argues that Bold Line Geometric is related to the Desert Abstract style of northwestern Mexico and the American Southwest, probably dates to the Late Prehistoric, and probably is indicative of groups intrusive to the Lower Pecos. Boyd (1998b:102-103) notes that geometric forms are present in the context of Pecos River Style panels, and suggests that the geometric patterns described by Turpin may simply be a depiction of entoptic phenomena. Entoptic phenomena are visual sensations originating from within the structure of the optic system at any point from the eyeball to the cortex of the brain. These sensations, which are seen by the affected individual as geometric patterns, are commonly induced by trance states, a key component of shamanic ritual. Therefore Bold Line Geometric may not be a separate style, but instead a motif within the previously identified styles. The most temporally recent style, identified as the Historic Style, is characterized by the presence of Old World animals and depictions of Spanish conquistadors. It is associated with Native American groups that lived in or passed through the area after European contact.

Particularly in the case of hunter-gatherers, sites often consist of the remains of redundant activities on different landforms. Thus, a site type may refer to the physical content of the site, such as a burned rock midden, or it may refer to activities carried out at the site, such as a bison-drive or kill site. It can also may refer to the site's position on the landscape, such as rockshelter or terrace sites (e.g., Bement 1989). For example, a burned rock midden may occur as a site type in an upland setting at the head of a canyon, as a feature in a stratified alluvial terrace site within a canyon, or as a feature in a rockshelter. Pearce and Jackson (1933:28) reported seven "sotol pits," the earth ovens that leave an accumulation of FCR commonly referred to as burned rock middens, in Fate Bell Shelter. In addition, Black (1997:395) demonstrated that burned rock middens are a composite of several feature types. Given that site types refer to different subject categories and that a single site is often comprised of a blend of feature types, assigning a site type is clearly a judgment call, and the criteria for making the judgement have not been explicitly stated in many previous surveys.

There is a need, therefore, to address the issue of site types in the region, and to establish a consistent method of assigning meaningful labels to sites for reference purposes. As Thomas (1988:167-168) has pointed out, the archeological site concept is best for bookkeeping, especially for management purposes, and is not so well suited for research purposes. Yet, the necessity of assigning site types for management purposes cannot be overlooked, and the research design will attempt to devise a system of site types that provides adequate descriptors.

Cultural Chronology

Chronology of the lower Pecos region has received much attention   a result of excellent preservation, an influx of research funds associated with construction of Amistad Reservoir, and the presence of deeply stratified sites associated with the Rio Grande, the Devils, and the Pecos Rivers. Turpin (1991) recorded 268 radiocarbon ages within or immediately adjacent to the lower Pecos River region on the United States' side of the border. Only limited research has been conducted in the Burro Mountains of Mexico.

Archeological research in the project area and surrounding regions has been primarily devoted to establishing a cultural-chronological framework. Deeply stratified alluvial terrace sites have provided the basis of well-documented artifact sequences for the Lower Pecos. Two of these sites have been excavated and reported: the Devils Mouth site at the junction of the Devils River and the Rio Grande (Johnson 1964), and Arenosa Shelter at the junction of the Pecos River and the Rio Grande (Dibble and Lorrain 1967). Chronology of the lower Pecos area has been divided into the traditional Paleoindian to Historic period scheme. Subperiods, originally developed by Dibble (1970), were based on the ^{14}C sequence at Arenosa Shelter. Later research considered other variables such as perishable material culture, subsistence, mortuary practices, and rock art stylistic changes (Bement 1989; Turpin 1995). An alternative chronology proposed by Shafer (1986:71-73) subdivides the sequence into five arbitrary intervals primarily based on subsistence technology within the region. A simplified cultural sequence based on previous chronologies is presented in the following discussion (Table 3.2).

Paleoindian Period (14,500–8500 B.P.). The earliest manifestations of human occupation in the region are poorly understood. Clovis and Folsom points have been recovered from undated surface contexts in southern Texas (Hester 1995:434). Burned bone of extinct vertebrate fauna was recovered from Bone Bed I at Bonfire Shelter (41VV218), but no stone tools were documented from this level (Dibble and Lorrain 1968). At Cueva Quebrada (41VV162A), burned Pleistocene mammal bones with butchering marks were recovered in association with 10 chipped stone flakes and a Clear Fork gouge. Charcoal from the same context as the burned bone yielded dates ranging between 12,000 to 14,300 B.P. (Turpin 1991). Although Clear Fork gouges are early tools, the temporal connection between these early dates and the tools is at best tenuous, and confirmation of such an early occupation awaits better data.

The archeological record verifies the presence of humans in the lower Pecos River region by 10,000 B.P. In Bone Bed 2 at Bonfire Shelter, extinct bison bones were recovered along with Folsom and Plainview dart points (Turpin 1991). This same deposit contained butchered remains totaling between 120 200 *Bison antiquus*, an extinct species. These animals were stampeded over a cliff into the canyon below, and butchering marks are clearly visible on many of the bones. *Bison antiquus* bones were also recovered from the middle levels of Cueva Quebrada and the lowest level of Arenosa Shelter, both of which are roughly contemporaneous with Bone Bed 2.

Around 9,000 years ago, distinct changes in the lifeways of Paleoindian groups began to emerge, as evidenced by artifactual evidence. Dart point styles became more localized and diverse. Numerous Angostura and Golondrina points, typical of the late Paleoindian period, have been recovered from the lower Pecos, Rio Grande Plains, and the plains of northeastern Mexico (Epstein 1969; Hester 1995; Turpin 1995). The large animals of the Pleistocene had become extinct, and the Late Paleoindian subsistence economy emphasized smaller game and more plant foods. This is best illustrated by analysis of a well-preserved hearth dating to 9000 B.P. in Baker Cave. The hearth contained 16 plant taxa, 11 mammalian taxa, six fish, and 18 reptiles (Hester 1983). The plant taxa are consistent with the vegetation of a semiarid savanna, quite similar to modern-day floral conditions. Although Bryant and Holloway (1985)

Table 3.2. Diagnostic artifacts of Lower Pecos regional cultural chronologies.

Years B.P.	Period (Turpin 1991, 1995)	Subperiod (Turpin 1991)	Interval (Shafer 1986)	Typical Diagnostics
0–350	Historic		Historic (400–150 B.P.)	Metal arrows
ca. 450	Protohistoric	Infierno (ca. 450 B.P.)		Stemmed arrow points, steeply beveled end-scrapers, ceramics
1320–450	Late Prehistoric	Flecha (1320–450 B.P.)	Comstock (1000–400 B.P.)	Scallorn, Perdiz, Livermore, Toyah
		Blue Hills (2300–1300 B.P.)		Ensor, Frio
		Flanders (ca. 2,300 B.P.)		Marcos, Shumla
3000–1000	Late Archaic	Cibola (3150–2300 B.P.)	Devils (3000–1000 B.P.)	Montell, Castroville, Marshall, Shumla
		San Felipe (4100–3200 B.P.)		Langtry, Val Verde, Arledge, Almagre
6000–3000	Middle Archaic	Eagle Nest (5500–4100 B.P.)	Pandale (5000–3000 B.P.)	Pandale
		Viejo (8900–5500 B.P.)	Baker (8500–5000 B.P.)	Baker, Bandy, Bell, Early Triangular
9000–6000	Early Archaic			
9800–8000	Late Paleoindian	Oriente (9400–8800 B.P.)	Golondrina (9000–8000 B.P.)	Angostura, Golondrina
			Folsom/Plainview (10,000–9000 B.P.)	Folsom, Plainview
11,000–9800		Bonfire (10,700–9800 B.P.)	Clovis (11,000–10,000 B.P.)	Clovis
14,500–11,900	Paleoindian	Aurora		None

demonstrated that the environment is rapidly warming during this period, it is quite likely that the region was already experiencing modern climatic conditions by about 9,000 years ago.

Early Archaic (8500–6000 B.P.). The combination of a semiarid climate, deep canyons, and dry rockshelters in the lower Pecos River region has created perfect conditions for the best preserved records of Archaic cultures during the middle Holocene in North America. Both coiled and plaited basketry and various tool forms   including oval unifacial tools, manos, metates, and bedrock mortars   have been documented. Cordage made from lechuguilla and yucca was utilized in nets, snares, tools, and sandals. The technology of basketry and sandal manufacture was so similar to that documented at sites in northern Mexico that affiliation with groups to the south and west in Coahuila has been postulated (Andrews and Adovasio 1980; McGregor 1992).

During the Early Archaic, rockshelter occupation became widespread in the lower Pecos River region. At Hinds Cave in Val Verde County, shelter activity areas were well defined, as indicated by the presence of a latrine area, a floored area made of prickly-pear pads, grass-lined pits, and oven areas surrounded by burned rock refuse (Lord 1984; Shafer and Bryant 1977). Projectile points characteristic of the area include Early Corner-Notched, Early Stemmed, and Early Barbed, as well as Baker and Bandy point types.

Two types of mobilary art are known from the Early Archaic - painted pebbles (Parsons 1986) and clay figurines (Shafer 1975). Painted pebbles are thought to represent human figures, usually feminine. Clay figurines have exaggerated female attributes, but are typically headless (Shafer 1975). Burial customs during the early Archaic are poorly known; however, a population of 21 individuals was recovered from Seminole Sink, a vertical-shaft cave associated with the Seminole Canyon drainage (Turpin 1988). All age groups and sexes were given the same type of burial, suggesting little social stratification.

Tools typical of the early Archaic included Early Corner-Notched points such as Bell and Andice types, sequent flake unifaces, and Clear Fork bifaces and unifaces, which were most likely woodworking tools. These appear in deposits that date to the late Paleoindian/Early Archaic periods, and have been recovered from numerous sites, including Baker Cave in the lower Pecos River region (Turner and Hester 1999) and the Richard Beene site in south-central Texas (Thoms 1992).

Middle Archaic (6000-3000 B.P.). As populations continued to grow and became more circumscribed, the people became increasingly reliant upon small animals and a greater variety of plant resources (Hester 1980). In the lower Pecos River region, the accepted diagnostic tool for the onset of the Middle Archaic is the Pandale dart point. Other stone-tool markers of the period include Langtry and Val Verde points.

A definitive marker of Early to Middle Archaic subsistence technology is the increased presence of earth ovens utilizing rocks as heating elements. By 6000 B.P., evidence from Hinds Cave in the lower Pecos River region demonstrates that earth ovens with rock heating elements were being utilized to bake lechuguilla (*Agave lechuguilla*) and sotol (*Dasylirion texanum*) (Dering 1999; Shafer and Bryant 1977). Similar ovens have been recorded at 5000 B.P. in Baker Cave by Brown (1991), who considers their presence to be an indication of a shift to less-desirable plant resources requiring more intensive labor input.

By 4000 B.P., Archaic cultures demonstrated increased regional diversity (Turpin 1995). Population densities increased as indicated by higher numbers of both "upland" and "lowland" sites in the lower Pecos River region (Marmaduke 1978). The apparent population increase was accompanied by the appearance of a complex, polychrome pictographic art form, termed the Pecos River Style, which is also considered a hallmark of the Middle Archaic in the lower Pecos River region (Kirkland and Newcomb 1967). These pictographs depict anthropomorphic (human-like), therianthropic (part human, part animal), and theriomorphic (animal-like) figures resembling deer, mountain lions, fishes, birds, humans, and many enigmatic figures. Anthropomorphic characters are often adorned with feathers, wings, and antlers, and are depicted holding plants, atlatls, darts, sticks, and pouches (Turpin 1994). These figures are believed to have been associated with shamanic rituals, and have been specifically linked to spiritual transformation of the participants (Boyd 1996, 1998b). Recent formal analyses of Pecos River Style rock art sites have demonstrated that some represent single panels of work depicting specific types of rituals (Boyd 1996; 1998a; Boyd and Dering 1996).

Late Archaic (3000–1200 B.P.). At least two distinct subsistence and environmental shifts may have occurred during the 2,000-year span of the Late Archaic. The onset of the Late Archaic in the lower Pecos River region is marked by the return of bison into the region (Bement 1989; Turpin 1995). Bryant and Holloway (1985) documented a mesic interval marked by spikes in pine and grass pollen. This interval coincides with Bone Bed III at Bonfire Shelter, which contained over 800 modern bison (*Bison bison*) individuals dated to 2600 B.P. (Dibble and Lorrain 1968). Remains of bison have been recovered from similar (but poorly dated) contexts in Eagle Cave, Arenosa Shelter, Castle Canyon, and Skyline Shelter (Turpin 1995). The environment of the period has been interpreted as cooler and wetter, promoting the growth of grasslands which allowed bison to return to the region. Dibble and Lorrain (1968) and Turpin (1995) argue that the influx of central Texas dart point styles (Montell, Ensor, Frio, Marshall, Castroville), the entry of a different "fully developed" Red Linear rock art type, and a perceived shift to open site habitation meet the conditions of a horizon, representing an in-migration of plains hunters.

Bison bone is rare in Late Archaic contexts, and plant assemblages do not register detectable vegetation changes between the Middle and Late Archaic, which include Baker Cave (Chadderdon 1983), Hinds Cave (Dering 1979; Lord 1984), and Conejo Shelter (Alexander 1974). Arguments for the return of grasslands during a mesic interval are weak, primarily because studies in southern Texas and eastern Africa indicate that woody vegetation in a savannah should increase during a period of higher effective moisture (cf. Archer 1995). Pollen data, which consist of relative frequencies from questionable contexts, may indicate the opposite   a slightly drier period favoring rhizomatous grasses over woody vegetation. Therefore, it is quite possible that the Plains region experienced drier conditions that encouraged a southward migration of some animals into the Lower Pecos River region. Nevertheless, the vegetation of immediate locales around the canyonlands would have been edaphically controlled   that is, large areas of bedrock would have remained exposed and shallow soils would have been widespread across canyonlands in which the study area is located. In addition, the canyons may have provided moist refugia for plants even during dry periods; therefore, regional climatic changes may not be detectable in rockshelter deposits.

During the final 1,000 years of the Late Archaic, a steady increase in aridity is implied by a drop in percentages of grass and tree pollen and by the disappearance of bison from archeological deposits (Bryant and Holloway 1985; Turpin 1995). Inception of this time period, termed the Flanders phase by Turpin (1991, 1995), is marked by presence of the Shumla point type. Because the Shumla point has been recovered from Cueva de la Zona in Mexico, Turpin (1991) maintains that people from the plains of Coahuila and the surrounding mountains moved into the lower Pecos River region following the withdrawal of bison hunters.

The final subperiod attributed to the Late Archaic of the lower Pecos River region is the Blue Hills, best marked by a change in mortuary practices. This change is represented by a shift to bundle burials in dry rockshelters. Coprolite studies suggest that sotol and yucca were important dietary resources (Bryant 1974; Sobolik 1991). These data are solely derived from two rockshelter sites and should not be considered to represent a complete image of regional land use, but rather a snapshot of place and time.

A perceived shift to more intensive plant processing during the latter part of the Late Archaic is argued based on the presence of burned rock middens both inside and outside rockshelters (Brown 1991; Saunders 1986). Analysis of plant materials from a ring-shaped burned rock midden dating to the Blue Hills subperiod (1820 B.P.) in Hinds Cave noted 35 plant species. Although the heated rock was primarily utilized to pit-bake sotol and lechuguilla, other very important plant resources recovered from the midden context included prickly pear (tuna and nodes) and mesquite (beans and seeds) (Dering 1999).

Late Prehistoric/Protohistoric (1300–500 B.P.). The Late Prehistoric period is marked by the appearance of arrow points and presumably by use of the bow and arrow (Hester 1995; Turpin 1995). In the lower Pecos River region, the earliest appearance of arrow points, the diagnostic artifact of the period, occurs around 1380 B.P. at Stratum 2A in Arenosa Shelter (Turpin 1991). To the south in Nuevo Leon, arrow points date to 1050 B.P. at La Calsada (Nance 1992), and to around 1200 B.P. at Cueva de la Zona. Many well-excavated sites in the lower Pecos region do not contain Late Prehistoric deposits, either due to changes in settlement patterns or to destruction of upper deposits by artifact hunters. Point types typical of the period in the lower Pecos include a variety of stemmed and unstemmed types, including Scallorn, Perdiz, Livermore, and Toyah (see Table 3.2).

The increase of ring- or crescent-shaped burned rock middens at open sites in upland settings within the lower Pecos River region attests to an intensification of lechuguilla and sotol processing (Dibble and Prewitt 1967; Greer 1968). Late Prehistoric burial customs included flexed interments, cremations, secondary disposal in vertical-shaft caves, and cairn burials. The Red Monochrome art style, some examples perhaps depicting bows and arrows, may be linked to this time period (Turpin 1991).

Both the Infierno and the Toyah phases are archeological constructs that previously have been assumed to identify two different groups. In central and southern Texas, the Toyah horizon, dated between A.D. 1250 to 1600, represents the best-documented archaeological manifestation of the Late Prehistoric period. It is associated with deer and particularly bison hunting (Black 1986; Johnson 1994). Perdiz arrow points and bone-tempered pottery, small end-scrapers, flake knives, beveled knives, perforators made on flakes, marine shell, and mussel shell typify assemblages from this horizon. The apparent emphasis on hunting exemplified by the tool kit suggests a reliance on more easily accessed food resources that do not require significant time or energy for processing. Therefore, it follows that these resources, most likely bison, may have returned to the region, thus bringing about this marked change in land use.

The Infierno phase of the lower Pecos River region is defined by stemmed arrow points, beveled end-scrapers, two- and four-beveled knives, as well as plain brownware and bone-tempered ceramics (Bement and Turpin 1987; McClurkan 1968). Settlements have been recorded only on promontories and are marked by circular stone alignments interpreted as tipi rings (Bement 1989; Turpin and Bement 1989). The Infierno phase artifact assemblage is comparable to the Toyah phase of central and southern Texas, and is interpreted as representing an influx of outsiders coinciding with the return of bison during a mesic interval within Protohistoric and early Historic times (Turpin 1995). Definition of the Infierno phase is based on site type and artifact descriptions with no radiocarbon ages or other means of dating the sites. As a result, age estimates for the Infierno phase of A.D. 1500 1780 are based on speculation.

A recent synthesis in connection with excavations conducted in the San Felipe Springs area suggests that these two phases may simply represent slight geographic or temporal variation within the same culture (Mehalchick and Boyd 1999:155). Comparison of the Infierno and Toyah phases illuminates the fact that only two fundamental differences separate these two archeological constructs. First, Perdiz points provide a defining diagnostic characteristic of the Toyah phase but have not been directly associated with Infierno phase sites. Second, stone circles, thought to be associated with temporary structures, have been described at Infierno sites but not for Toyah phase sites. In contrast, the two phases share many similar aspects of material culture, including bone-tempered pottery, scrapers, beveled knives, and the presence of arrow points.

Because our sample size of sites attributable to either the Infierno or Toyah phases remains small, dating these phases remains problematic. Of the twelve sites in the Lower Pecos region that have yielded bone-tempered pottery, six have contained Perdiz points, eight have contained other arrow point types, and five have contained both Perdiz and other arrow point types, both stemmed and notched. Mehalchick and Boyd (1999:156) point out that although stone alignments/circles are associated with Infierno phase sites, there are only two published accounts of sites identified with this phase and both are located on deflated landforms and no radiocarbon dates are available. A similar dearth of information exists for the Toyah phase of the Lower Pecos. Only three sites on alluvial terraces with discrete Toyah phase components have been excavated in the region Javelina Bluff (McClurkan 1968), Devil's Mouth (Johnson 1964; Sorrow 1968), and most recently San Felipe Springs (Mehalchick et al. 1999). Of these components, only the San Felipe Springs site has been radiocarbon dated to A.D. 1295 1420 (Beta-116160) (Mehalchick et al. 1999:178).

The small number of excavated Infierno and Toyah phase sites from the region, and the problems with obtaining accurate dates for them begs for more study of this most interesting time period. Mehalchick and Boyd (1999) conclude that there are two possible explanations for the considerable overlap in material culture characteristics between the Toyah and Infierno sites. First, the the Infierno phase may actually represent a very late, intrusive Protohistoric Plains culture that has a lifestyle and material culture very similar to the Toyah culture. Or, alternatively, it may simply represent a geographic or temporal continuum, a later manifestation, of the Toyah culture in the Lower Pecos region (Mehalchick and Boyd 1999:157).

Historic (500 B.P.–Present). At the beginning of this period, Cabeza de Vaca was the first European to enter the Rio Grande Plains and coastal plain regions of Texas (Favata and Fernandez 1993), and Castaño de Sosa was the first European to traverse the lower Pecos River region (Schroeder and Matson 1965). Spanish accounts often describe the Lower Pecos region as uninhabited; however, illegal slaving expeditions that preceded de Sosa's entry may have encouraged the Indians to avoid all contact with Europeans. For a review of historic Indian groups in the lower Pecos River region, see Labadie (1994).

Written records from the Protohistoric and early Historic periods (ca. A.D. 1500 1750) indicate that the region was populated by hunter-gatherer groups. No plant husbandry was noted by early observers. Cabeza de Vaca's observations emphasize heavy reliance on plant foods, especially roots (unidentified), prickly pear, and mesquite (Thoms 1997a). Further west and south into Mexico, lechuguilla (*mezcal*) was an important staple. Reliance on mesquite, lechuguilla, grass seed, prickly-pear tuna and nopales, and roots has been noted in historic records from northern Mexico, including Nuevo Leon and western Coahuila (Griffen 1969:110). Thoms (1997a) notes that when Cabeza de Vaca lived in the Rio Grande Plains and crossed southwestern North America, he seldom traveled a day without observing a settlement or other people, implying a fairly high population density. This density was not observed by subsequent travelers, likely a result of depopulation due to the introduction of European diseases.

A major factor influencing our understanding of historic native populations of the region is that frequently, these geographic ranges of populations overlapped into southern and central Texas and the lower Pecos. Secondly, historic groups were widely displaced by contemporary Spanish frontier expansion (Hester 1989). Local population ranges were also influenced by intrusions of Apache, Comanche, and their allies from the north and west.

From the beginning of the Spanish Colonial period (1590 1821) to the era of Texas statehood (1865 1880), Native Americans in Texas have been part of a dynamic, often volatile, relationship with Europeans. Although populations of Coahuiltecan-speaking groups were reduced by European diseases during the period of Spanish contact, families that can directly trace their ancestry to the Spanish Colonial period are still present and active in the San Antonio area (Thoms 1997b:204). Labadie (1994:12-17) summarized major historical periods for the lower Pecos region of Texas, the role of Native Americans during the Historic period, as well as Euro-American ranching and the railroad industry that entered the region in the nineteenth century.

PREHISTORIC ECONOMY AND SETTLEMENT

Current understanding of adaptation in the lower Pecos area holds that the inhabitants were strictly hunters and gatherers throughout the entire history of occupation (Shafer 1989:27). The character of the environment, both in terms of resource availability and quantity, coupled with residential mobility, fostered an egalitarian, band-level social organization with low population densities. According to Shafer (1989:27-28), the most common settlements were open-air camps, with sheltered areas sought in certain times of need. The variety of archeological sites known to occur in the lower Pecos (cf. Black 1989) could have easily been created during a single occupational episode. The range of site types that are known to exist in this region include rockshelters with deep midden deposits, open middens located on alluvial or colluvial terraces, burned rock middens, hearth fields, rock alignments, quarries, burial sites, and rock art locations (Bement 1989; Shafer 1989).

Overview of Regional Economy and Diet

The rich archeological record of the Lower Pecos region has provided much data for the reconstruction of prehistoric hunter-gatherer economy in the region. The economy of the Archaic period has been approached from the viewpoint of animal procurement (Lord 1984), plant gathering (Dering 1999), coprolites and diet (Bryant 1974; Sobolik 1991, 1996; Williams-Dean 1978), midden analysis (Alexander 1974), bioarcheology (Marks et al. 1988; Reinhard et al. 1989), and site distribution (Marmaduke 1978; Saunders 1986, 1992; Turpin 1995).

Brown (1991) proposes that the onset of the Hypsithermal, a period of warmer, drier climate lasting from about 8,000 4,500 B.P, coincided with an increase in diet-breadth and the advent of a least-risk economic strategy, characterized by the processing of lechuguilla, sotol, and yucca in earth ovens. Small-scale, earth-oven processing commenced around 5000 B.P. as a response to dietary stress during temporary food shortages, probably during the winter (Brown 1991:123). Sobolik (1996:203, 211) maintains that agave, yucca, sotol, and prickly pear were used as staples, particularly during times of subsistence stress. These resources were used within the context of a varied diet that included several other plant species, small and large mammals, reptiles, and fish (Sobolik 1991, 1996).

Bioarcheological studies of the region indicate the effects of a diet very high in carbohydrates, suggesting that the population did not have easy access to adequate fat and protein resources. Because large game, if available, are a more efficient means of procuring sustenance than small game (see Kelly 1995:88), one would expect evidence of large game(deer, pronghorn, and bison) in well-preserved habitation sites in the region. In fact, the faunal analysis from Hinds Cave revealed an assemblage dominated by small game, mostly rodents and rabbits (Lord 1984). The Early Archaic burial population (N=21) from Seminole Sink, the largest single regional burial population studied to date, shows that adult hyperostosis rates approached those of maize agriculturalists. The presence of Harris lines and enamel hypoplasias may indicate short-term, seasonal stress (Reinhard et al. 1989), and the high rate of dental caries meets or exceeds that of maize agriculturalists (Marks et al. 1988:116-117; Reinhard et al. 1989). The population was heavily dependent on carbohydrates to the extent that individuals suffered from excessive caries, dental attrition, and possibly iron deficiency (Marks et al. 1988; Reinhard et al. 1989).

Recent experimental studies and botanical analyses of earth ovens have demonstrated that Archaic period earth ovens in the Lower Pecos region would have rather small-scale caloric yields. Intensive cropping would had led to quick depletion of lechuguilla and sotol fields, and the large quantities of wood needed to fire the ovens would have exhausted local fuel supplies. The tremendous amount of refuse generated by lechuguilla and sotol processing in earth ovens produces a rapidly accumulating midden, creating the impression of an economy driven by plant resources that in reality do not produce that many calories. The overwhelming archeological visibility of earth-oven debris may have resulted in overestimates of group size, length of stay, and in underestimates of mobility (Dering 1999).

Subsistence/Settlement Models

Several models of subsistence and settlement have been proposed for the lower Pecos River region and adjacent northeastern Mexico. Residential mobility has been viewed to be affected primarily by the distribution of surface water sources. For example, an early adaptive model proposed for Coahuila and the adjacent portion of the lower Pecos was developed by W.W. Taylor, and was referred to as the concept of "tethered nomadism" (Taylor 1964:201). This model of settlement and subsistence is based upon small, highly mobile bands of egalitarian hunter-gatherers exploiting a given area. Their degree of nomadism and their routes were governed by the location and dependability of available sources of water. This model is quite appropriate and testable for the area west of the lower Pecos canyonlands, such as the lands between the Rio Grande and the Burro Mountains in Coahuila (Bement 1989:74-75).

Bement (1989) suggested that this model is not entirely appropriate for the canyonlands area due to the stability and abundance of available supplies of water, specifically the Rio Grande and the Pecos and Devils rivers. There is direct evidence supporting a less nomadic lifestyle during the Middle Archaic; specifically, increased component counts based on regional survey and excavation, deep cultural deposits in dry caves and rockshelters, and extended occupations of these sites with little indication of seasonal occupational variation (Bement 1989:75; Marmaduke 1978).

In addition to Taylor's (1964) and Bement's (1989) general statements, four subsistence models have examined change in adaptive responses through time. One of the earliest models emphasizes the study of subsistence remains, and proposed a sequence of very gradual change within a relatively stable hunting and gathering lifeway (see Kirkland and Newcomb 1967; Shafer 1976, 1981, 1986, 1989). Turpin (1990, 1995) proposed a different version of this model based upon a series of both abrupt and gradual changes within a mobile hunting and gathering lifeway. Turpin's (1995:543) model is based on multiple lines of data, such as rock art, mortuary customs, and settlement patterns, and less upon subsistence remains.

Dering (1999) has recently proposed a third model of subsistence and settlement that utilizes archeological data examined within the context of regional ecology. In a region with high interannual rainfall variation, hunter-gatherer subsistence organization and territorial boundaries may have been fluid, adjusting to seasonal or annual changes in the physical or social environment (Hitchcock and Bartram 1998:33; Simms 1987:89; Thomas 1983:21). Depending on conditions in a given year or even a given decade, a specific area would be visited at different seasons or utilized for different activities (cf. Binford 1982). This is supported by the fact that rockshelter sites contain flower and fruit fragments representing every season of the year (Alexander 1974; Dering 1998; Irving 1966; Williams-Dean 1978). Seasonal data were previously thought to represent extended residence. Rainfall can be remarkably localized in the region (Norwine 1995), especially in years of drought, forcing hunter-gatherers to map onto continually changing distributions in regional resource abundance (Binford 1980). Under these conditions, the concept of a seasonal round (Shafer 1981; Sobolik 1996) does not provide a good fit with the ecological or archeological evidence, where extreme interannual variation in rainfall would require extreme adjustments to subsistence strategies. Because refuse from earth ovens has been demonstrated to accumulate at a very rapid rate, deep deposits in rockshelters or burned rock middens give the illusion of long-term residential stays in the region. Therefore, one may infer a type of residential mobility different from that anticipated by the concept of tethered nomadism, and a level of mobility higher than that suggested by the concept of residential rockshelters or canyons (Alexander 1974; Shafer 1981; Taylor 1964). In the Lower Pecos region, mobility was not tethered to water, but rather was governed by the rapid depletion of local food resources. Archeological and experimental data support the argument that residential mobility remained high and group size remained small throughout the Archaic period (Dering 1999).

Saunders (1992) has provided the only study of subsistence organization that is explicitly based on survey data. Saunders' (1992) study of technological organization in the area around Hinds Cave demonstrates the presence of hunting sites in upland hilly areas away from the canyons, and a combination of hunting/plant-gathering sites within and adjacent to the canyons. Although Saunders (1992) research represents an excellent example of the application of survey data to land-use studies, its scope is limited to a small area. It does, however, provide a reliable database that can be combined with future comparable studies throughout the region.

Therefore, subsistence/settlement models suffer from a lack of reliable regional survey data. Although subsistence studies are able to draw upon the detailed analyses of well-preserved rockshelter deposits, archeological survey data have only been able to give a general impression of the regional archeological landscape. One of the weakest links in most of the subsistence/settlement models is that they do not incorporate specific data sets from archeological surveys conducted in the region. Thus, an adequate survey database would serve to fill one of the most glaring data gaps in the region.

DATA DEFICIENCIES

Despite the intensity of study in the region, there are several data deficiencies in both cultural chronology and settlement/subsistence studies in the region. Although Turpin (1991) has been able to assemble a well considered chronological sequence for the region, the need remains to apply state-of-the-art dating techniques to sites which have been adequately reported. Most excavations in the region were conducted over 25 years ago, and few of these have been reported in detail. As a result, most of the radiocarbon sequence consists of uncorrected dates obtained over 20 years ago from unidentified plant material. The error ranges for many of the dates are very broad, and many dates are questionable due to problems with stratigraphy and reporting (Turpin 1991). Stratigraphic context of the dated samples is often problematic because they come from rockshelter sites that often present difficult depositional sequences. Sites located on alluvial terraces provide an ideal setting for establishing cultural sequences, but only two have been the subject of large-scale excavations – Arenosa Shelter and the Devils Mouth site (Dibble 1967; Johnson 1964; Sorrow 1968).

The paleoenvironmental record is based on limited data obtained from a single site, Hinds Cave, and from cursory studies of several rockshelters which have never been fully reported. Pollen analyses at Arenosa Shelter and the Devils Mouth site were conducted over 30 years ago, and constitute a data set that has been inadequately reported because it lacked concentration values (Vaughn Bryant, personal communication 2000). Further, the canyons from which most of the data are reported constitute refugia for vegetation and are not very sensitive to regional climatic change. Geomorphological studies constitute a data set that would complement both environmental and cultural historical research. Prior to impoundment of the reservoir, only a cursory study of the regional geoarcheology at Arenosa Shelter had been conducted (Patton and Dibble 1982). Other than a preliminary study of alluvial deposits at 41VV661, just below Amistad Dam on the Rio Grande (Gufstason and Collins 1998), no other recent geomorphological or geoarcheological studies have been completed in the region. Therefore, although detailed descriptive studies of a well-preserved material record are available, they lack an adequate temporal context.

Subsistence/settlement models suffer from similar data gaps. Each one of the preceding settlement/subsistence models has a basis in archeological survey, yet archeological survey is one of the weakest data sets in the region. Although subsistence studies are able to draw upon the detailed analyses of well-preserved rockshelter deposits, archeological survey data have only been able to give a general impression of the regional archeological landscape. One of the weakest links in most of the subsistence/settlement models is that they do not incorporate specific data sets from archeological surveys conducted in the region. Saunders' (1992) argument for upland hunting and canyon hunting/plant gathering is the only study that incorporates a survey data set. While it provides an excellent example of how survey data may be utilized to address a research design, Saunders' research is an explicit study of technological organization and is limited in scope to a small area of the region. Thus, an adequate survey database would serve to fill one of the most glaring data gaps in the region.

A REVIEW OF SURVEY METHODS

Although there are many problems with regional survey data, one primary reason for the lack of survey-based research is that surveys have not been conducted with long-term synthesis of multiple data sets as a goal. Most of the existing separate data sets are incompatible, and the research potential for survey data remains largely untapped. The fact that survey data have yet to be assembled provides a compelling reason for the National Park Service to provide such a data set from the studies that have been conducted in and around the Amistad NRA. The next section of this report provides a history of previous survey research and method in the region.

Archeological survey in the region has a history spanning almost 45 years. A review of this long history is presented below for several reasons. First, we need to understand the level of survey coverage in the region before the reservoir was filled since subsistence/settlement systems must have been affected by the deep canyons that have been covered by the reservoir. Second, it is necessary to establish the level of comparability of survey data gleaned from several different field projects conducted between the 1950s and 1990s. This review attempts to focus on four main aspects of each survey   coverage, field methods, site definitions, and site types.

Formal survey of the lower Pecos River region began in 1958 when the first reconnaissance of the proposed Diablo Reservoir was conducted. Survey and salvage excavation continued in the area under the direction of the Texas Archeological Salvage Project (TASP) at the University of Texas at Austin. The TASP surveys were of a smaller scale than the original reconnaissance, and were not intended to provide a complete inventory of archeological sites within the proposed flood pool of the reservoir. Small-scale survey of several areas slated for development around the reservoir was conducted by the National Park Service in 1973. Several other minor surveys were conducted within the boundaries of Amistad NRA between 1987 and 1990. Major survey of the reservoir area languished for almost two decades until the current studies were undertaken. A list of previous major surveys, the area covered, and the number of sites documented is presented in Table 3.3.

Diablo Reservoir Survey

The first large-scale survey in the reservoir area was conducted under the auspices of the Archeological Salvage Program Field Office, National Park Service, Austin, Texas. Field reconnaissance on the United States' side was conducted between January   early March 1958 by John A. Graham and W.A. Davis, under the supervision of E.B. Jelks. F. González-Rul and W.W. Taylor, both of the Instituto Nacional de Antropología y Historia (INAH), surveyed the Mexican side of the reservoir area (González-Rul 1990; Graham and Davis 1958).

Graham and Davis (1958:9) stated that both funding and time allotted for the survey were insufficient for the area to be covered; therefore, emphasis was placed on large sites located primarily

Table 3.3. Previous large-scale surveys conducted in the lower Pecos River region.

Survey	Source	Area	Site Count	Site Density (sites/km^2)
Diablo Reservoir	Graham and Davis (1958)	231.8 km^2	251	1.08
Seminole Canyon State Park	Turpin (1982)	8.5 km^2	70	8.2
Devils River State Natural Area	Turpin and Davis (1993)	68.9 km^2	233	3.38
Hinds Ranch	Saunders (1992)	14.76 km^2	610	41.3
Blue Hills	Saunders (1992)	4.14 km^2	57	13.77

within the three main river canyons. They contacted local collectors and friendly landowners, found the largest sites, and recorded them. Known sites were revisited, and in many cases, aerial reconnaissance was conducted prior to pedestrian survey. In addition, a boat survey of the Rio Grande was conducted from the upper reaches of the reservoir area to the mouth of the Devils River. Although it is difficult to determine survey coverage, the report implies that pedestrian survey was quite limited. In fact, the authors admit that in order to adequately cover just the bluffs of the major canyons would have required at least two more months (Graham and Davis 1958).

Although the exact area of the initial survey is impossible to determine, the target area of the Amistad Reservoir covers approximately 57,292 acres (Labadie 1994:1). Graham and Davis stated that the surveyors covered approximately 70 percent of the total reservoir area, which is approximately 40,110 acres. Surveyors noted 251 sites, 63 from the Mexican side of the Rio Grande, and 188 from the United States' side (Graham and Davis 1958:82; Taylor 1958:87).

Survey on the Mexican side of the reservoir originally reported 63 sites, far fewer than were noted on the American side. Taylor (in Graham and Davis 1958:87) noted that far fewer surface artifacts, habitation sites, and pictographs were located on the Mexican side, but he does not provide an explanation for this discrepancy. The 1958 survey of the Mexican side of the reservoir was finally reported in some detail by González-Rul (1990), who conducted much of the field work for Taylor in 1958. The final report describes 68 archeological sites on the Mexican side of the reservoir area (González-Rul 1990:133; Taylor and Rul 1961).

Texas Archeological Survey Project

Following the survey conducted by Graham and Davis (1958), the next major survey was carried out by the Texas Archeological Salvage Project (TASP) of the University of Texas at Austin. TASP investigations consisted of a series of localized surveys focusing on limited areas within the proposed boundaries of the reservoir. In 1962, Parker Nunley directed the testing of four sites; during these investigations, incidental survey was conducted in the immediate vicinity of the tested sites. The sites 41VV3, 41VV82, 41VV215, and 41VV216 were situated throughout the reservoir area from the lower Devils River to Seminole Canyon. In 1963 and 1964, Mark Parsons surveyed the Bonfire Shelter area around Langtry (Elton R. Prewitt, personal communication 1998). These informal surveys were not published, but site forms on file at TARL confirm these activities.

In 1964, David Dibble conducted a survey of two areas around the lower reaches of the Devils and Pecos Rivers. Details of the survey method were not published (Dibble and Prewitt 1967); however, the authors did refer to how they approached the problem of survey coverage. Instead of concentrating efforts in the main streams, emphasis was placed on examining drainages away from the main canyons. The survey method was described as follows:

> In the process of surveying for sites in the entrenched canyons of the two rivers, it was soon noticed that many relatively small open sites were situated in the bottoms of, or bordering, the myriad of dry tributary canyons as well as on the tops of bluffs enclosing the primary canyons. Though few of these sites appear as though they would be informative on excavation (most occur on severely deflated surfaces), their gross surface characteristics and location seemed significant enough to record. Considerable attention was thus directed at walking out drainages away from the main canyons. Virtually all of the sites located will fall within the maximum (flood pool) anticipated elevations of the reservoir [Dibble and Prewitt 1967:5].

This statement of method says as much about the nature of the previous survey by Graham and Davis (1958) as it does about the TASP survey to which it actually refers. Previous surveys were not only limited to points lower than the flood pool, but were also primarily restricted to the main water courses. As implied by Dibble and Prewitt, very few areas located beyond the three main river canyons were surveyed during previous fieldwork. In addition, because survey was confined to elevations below the flood pool, most areas located just beyond the canyon rims were not examined.

As a result of their efforts, an additional 69 sites were reported and briefly described (Dibble and Prewitt 1967:8-39). As noted by Prewitt (personal communication 1998), Dibble was the first archeologist in the region to carefully examine some upland areas beyond the confines of the canyons, and the first to find and describe upland rock alignments in the region. However, descriptions of the rock alignments were not published.

In addition to the lack of survey in side canyons, it is possible that large tracts of land within the major river canyons were never thoroughly surveyed. During the TASP survey, access to the Kelly Ranch and Goodenough Springs, one the largest springs in Texas, was not granted. This locus likely represents one of the most intensively utilized areas in the lower Pecos River region, as well as within the immediate area of Amistad Reservoir. In addition to problems accessing property within the flood-pool area, upland access (i.e., access to areas beyond the limits of the narrow and deeply incised canyons) was extremely limited during all of these surveys (Elton Prewitt, personal communication 1998). This survey bias toward large sites located within or adjacent to canyons and major streams has been noted by others (Dymond 1976; Saunders 1992).

Archeological Assessment of Amistad NRA

The National Park Service conducted an assessment of cultural resources in the reservoir area in 1973, including a records search and a field survey of areas set aside to be developed for recreation around the reservoir (Anderson 1974). Beyond the statement that this was an intensive survey, survey field techniques are not provided in the report and the minimal definition of a site is not given. A list of 12 site types, however, was provided (Anderson 1974:14). The survey was conducted primarily for management purposes, but included an assessment of current holdings and data deficiencies.

> Perhaps most urgent in priorities is an intensive survey of all National Park Service owned land especially if additional lands are required at the Pecos River, Rough Canyon, and

Comstock development areas, and both Seminole and Mile Canyon Archeological Districts as suggested by the most recent Master Plan for Amistad National Recreation Area. This intensive survey should also include the intensive investigation on some privately owned lands which could offer important archeological information relating to the Amistad area in general. A survey of this nature could be added to previous archeological studies to provide data for a settlement pattern study for the Amistad region [Anderson 1974:36].

Anderson (1974) mentioned that data deficiencies include the excavation of open sites beyond the margins of canyons, many which are located within park boundaries. Fieldwork was conducted during this assessment within a series of relatively small parcels located in the Langtry, Pecos River, Comstock, Cow Creek, Diablo West, Diablo East, Lower Rio Grande, San Pedro, Long's Point, and Rough Canyon Development areas. Although the total size of all survey areas was reported to be 13.5 km^2 (3,300 acres), sizes of each parcel were not reported. Anderson (1974:9) noted that five additional sites were discovered, but did not state whether previously reported sites were located or revisited within his survey areas. Therefore, this survey is excluded from Table 3.3.

Seminole Canyon State Park Survey

Archeological reconnaissance of Seminole Canyon State Park was conducted as a surface pedestrian survey (Turpin 1982). It is implied, although not explicitly stated in the methods, that 100-percent coverage of the park was attempted. Transect spacing was dictated by local topography. Field crews walked along the contour lines formed by ascending limestone outcrops, which were altered by the presence of tributary canyons. As a result, spacing between surveyors was adjusted to suit changing factors of ground cover and topography (Turpin 1982:44).

Because it covered all of the upland area between the canyons, the Seminole Canyon State Park survey was much more inclusive than previous efforts. However, as investigators emphasized, the park itself did not include the headers of the main canyons, and was too small to be considered representative of the regional upland topography (Turpin 1982:9).

This was the first survey in the region that actually provided a specifically bounded site definition. Sites were defined as a locus of human activity reflected by " . . . the presence of features or of temporally or functionally diagnostic artifacts accompanied by other cultural material, sufficient to indicate a more than passing occupation" (Turpin 1982:46). Given the highly mobile nature of hunter-gatherer residence, the site definition used in the Seminole Canyon State Park survey defines only residential occupations. The Seminole Canyon State Park survey, however, is historically the first representation of a thorough pedestrian survey in the lower Pecos River region, although it occurred just beyond the boundaries of the Amistad Reservoir.

Hinds Ranch and Blue Hills Surveys

Surveys at Hinds Ranch and Blue Hills were conducted by Saunders (1986, 1992) in conjunction with excavation and analysis of Hinds Cave (41VV456). These two survey areas, located beyond the limits of the Amistad NRA about 12 km north of the Rio Grande, covered about 18.9 km^2. Saunders' (1986) effort is the most thorough survey effort conducted in the region, and stands as a model for future research-oriented survey. Both the survey method and the definition of a site are clearly described. In addition, the site definition is sufficiently inclusive to encompass both residential and small, special activity sites, allowing the full spectrum of hunter-gatherer activities to be examined in the context of a survey.

Saunders (1992:340) defined a site as an area containing at least more than one artifact within a diameter of 5 m, and an isolate as a locus that contained only a single artifact within a diameter of 5 m. Isolated flakes were not recorded. A site did not have to contain a feature, but most sites types described in his survey results did contain features. Site types included quarries, rockshelters, burned rock features (< 2 m diameter), burned rock middens (> 2 m diameter), burned rock scatters, and rock hearths. Because the survey included sites and isolates, Saunders (1992:340) specified the 10 artifact types he recorded during survey: projectile points, formal bifaces, preforms, choppers, bifacial scrapers, formal unifaces, modified flakes, denticulates, cores, and flakes.

Saunders' (1992:340) coverage of the area included tracts that followed the limestone outcrops in transects spaced 1 to 2 m apart. In areas that lacked clear landmarks, transects were marked with flagging tape. In upland areas, searches were conducted from lower to higher elevations in order to detect the effects of downslope erosion. This prevented the designation of artifacts that had traveled downslope from another locus as indicators of separate sites.

The survey recorded a total of 610 sites and 83 isolates on Hinds Ranch and 57 sites with 29 isolates in the Blue Hills survey area. Unlike other surveys conducted in the region, results of this survey reflect the material remains of plant and animal procurement activities, as well as residential locales and other activities, because the survey concentrated on low density sites and isolates.

Devils River State Natural Area Survey

The Texas Archeological Society conducted a field school in the Devils River State Natural Area (DRSNA), located along Dolan Creek about 30 km north of Amistad NRA. Although the survey was conducted beyond the boundaries of Amistad, it is mentioned here primarily because of the method used and results generated by that method. Covering 6,880 hectares (17,000 acres), this was the largest survey in the lower Pecos River region that was designed to cover both uplands and lowlands by encompassing several canyons and their associated interfluves (Turpin and Davis 1993:8). In comparison, Saunders' (1986, 1992) survey of Hinds Ranch and Blue Hills covered a combined area of 4,670 acres. The drawback to the survey is that it was conducted by a very large group of avocational archeologists over a very short time period   one week. Data gleaned from this survey should be treated as preliminary work.

In order to facilitate comparison, the six site types utilized in the DRSNA survey conformed to those used in the Seminole Canyon State Park Survey (Turpin and Davis 1993:8). It is assumed, although not directly stated, that the investigators used the same definition for a site that was used in the Seminole Canyon investigations. As such, defined sites would represent more intensively occupied loci and the survey would have overlooked procurement sites, as noted in the review of the Seminole Canyon State Park Survey. The DRSNA survey, combined with earlier efforts (Marmaduke and Whitsett 1975), documented 233 prehistoric and six historic sites in the area.

Previous Site Surveys and Site Definitions

Surveys based on the site concept usually provide a minimal definition for the types and quantities of material remains that constitute a site. Reasons given for this minimal definition are usually based on economics and other management decisions. For example, in the Seminole Canyon State Park survey, Turpin (1982:47) stated, "The decision to define site boundaries as specifically as possible from surficial indications was made in conjunction with TPWD in order to facilitate cultural resource management and Park development." The intent was to avoid describing Seminole Canyon State Park as a single site containing several loci of more densely distributed cultural materials.

Results of surveys conducted in the lower Pecos region (see Table 3.3) illustrate that how a site is defined affects the outcome of a survey project. The following two site definitions for regional surveys presented in the table provide an excellent example of how site definitions affect the data:

(1) Hinds Ranch/Blue Hills survey: "Any collection of more than one artifact, or a feature, located within a circular area of 5 m in diameter" (Saunders 1992:340).

(2) Seminole Canyon State Park survey: "Sites were defined on the basis of the presence of features or of temporally or functionally diagnostic artifacts accompanied by other cultural material, sufficient to indicate a more than passing use of the location" (Turpin 1982:46).

Saunders' (1992) minimal definition for a site is both more exact and more inclusive than the definition provided by Turpin (1982). Because Saunders' (1992) site definition is more inclusive   that is, it includes smaller sites   it would be expected that site density data resulting from the Hinds Ranch survey would be higher than site density data resulting from the Seminole Canyon survey.

The Hinds Ranch/Blue Hills survey sets a standard for the region in that it applies an explicit site definition and field protocol to two very different landforms within a limited geographic area. Because the two areas were assessed using the same crew and operating under the same field protocols, results of the survey accurately reflect site and artifact distributions in the region. Hinds Ranch is located between Lewis Canyon and Still Canyon, two tributary canyons of the Pecos River. By contrast, Blue Hills, a few kilometers to the north of Hinds Ranch, is an area located away from either canyons or major streams. Saunders (1992) found that site density in the canyon-dissected Hinds Ranch area was about three times greater than that in the upland Blue Hills.

When the survey conducted by Saunders (1992) is compared to the Seminole Canyon survey, the impact of site definitions is easily observable. Data from Hinds Ranch and Seminole Canyon State Park provide a good comparison because both areas are located along major canyon tributaries of major streams, which are analogous landforms. One would predict site density in these two areas to be similar; however, as noted in Table 3.3, site density from the Hinds Ranch section of Saunders (1992) survey is four times greater than site density from the Seminole Canyon State Park survey.

Site density figures derived from the Seminole Canyon State Park survey are even lower than the upland Blue Hills Survey. This is significant because the Blue Hills are a true upland area away from major canyons and associated resources; one would expect site density away from canyons to be much lower. Rather than being a real manifestation of the archeological record, it is likely that the disparity in site density between the Hinds Ranch/Blue Hills survey and the Seminole Canyon survey resulted from differing definitions of what constitutes an archeological site. Although the differing density figures may reflect the archeological record, we will never know until a consistent site definition is applied to regional surveys. Therefore, at the very least it is necessary to establish an explicit minimal site definition for survey projects, or in this case a series of surveys, so that results are consistent from project to project, and so that results may be applied to current and future research designs with some confidence in the data.

CONCLUSIONS

This review of regional archeology has focused on the importance of subsistence/settlement models in understanding foraging lifeways, and has emphasized the potential importance that survey data has in these models. It has addressed issues that must be considered when applying survey data to research questions. Previous surveys have had different approaches, different coverage, either unreported field methods or different field methods, and each exhibited variation in site typology and site definition. Although site definitions were provided for survey outside of Amistad NRA (Saunders 1992; Turpin 1982; Turpin and Davis 1993), none have been provided for survey within the Park. In addition, Saunders' (1992) survey was the only example that provided a systematic means of reporting surface artifacts. Finally, the pre-inundation survey was conducted prior to the advent of modern survey methods and did not cover large parts of the reservoir area.

Therefore, survey coverage within the boundaries of the Amistad NRA has been discontinuous and research designs have lacked rigor. This is primarily because most of the surveys occurred before detailed and modern survey methods were developed. Survey methods were inconsistent from one project to the next. Specifically, early surveys conducted within Amistad NRA lacked a well-developed research design stating the following objectives that are considered standard procedure in current survey methods:

(1) Explicitly stated coverage;
(2) A clear definition of what constitutes an archeological site;
(3) Explicitly stated transect intervals; and
(4) A consistently applied site typology.

Despite these shortcomings, the data are useful if the researcher carefully adjusts the resolution of the research questions to fit the relatively coarse resolution of the data. What must happen first, however, is the establishment of a consistent site typology for the region, as well as determination of an explicit definition of an archeological site. Once these tasks are accomplished, the data may be incorporated into a single large data set, with an understanding of its limitations. Further, new surveys may be conducted that are compatible with each other.

This review has provided an assessment of the archeological survey data available up to the inception of the SAIP and low-water surveys reported in the following chapter. The next section presents a research design which provides a framework for the synthesis of past and present survey data.

Chapter 4

RESEARCH DESIGN

The ultimate *research goal* of an archeological survey is to describe the signature of land use and document the patterns of human settlement (Feder 1997:42). The ultimate *management goal* of a site survey is to locate and record the distribution of archeological sites, describe their content, and eventually determine their eligibility for inclusion in the National Register of Historic Places, with a view toward the preservation of valuable archeological data. The immediate objective is to place a site in time and space, and to record its contents. Ultimately, survey data are incorporated within a management plan. In order to attain these goals, the archeologist usually focuses upon the discovery and description of archeological sites, their boundaries, and the material within them.

This chapter presents a research design that provides a framework for past and future survey in the region. The goal is to establish a consistent method for identifying and describing sites that will allow comparisons of survey results both within and outside of Amistad NRA. The chapter is divided into two parts. First, research and management goals of archeological survey are briefly summarized. Second, a site definition is provided, along with a site typology. This site typology has been entered into the ASMIS database and is used to categorize sites recorded by the surveys described in this report in Chapter 5.

RESEARCH OBJECTIVES

Research objectives typically consider two questions. First, what potential contribution to regional archeology can be provided by a survey conducted within the Amistad NRA? Building upon the first question, what kinds of data need to be gathered in order to realize that potential contribution?

Determination of settlement patterns is a primary research objective of most archeological surveys. Settlement pattern refers to the distribution of sites or activity loci across the landscape. Although several researchers have proposed that hunter-gatherers of the Lower Pecos region maintained a high level of residential mobility within large territories (Dering 1999; Sobolik 1996), there are no reliable survey data to conclusively support these ideas (see discussion of prehistoric economy in Chapter 2). Thus, one of the largest and most fundamental data gaps in the region is a clear understanding of settlement patterns. Future surveys in the Amistad NRA should be designed with the key research objective being to better document the distribution of archeological loci across the landscape.

Previous surveys conducted in the region can be used as a guide for research objectives within the Amistad NRA. The survey report authored by Turpin (1982) noted that the area covered by Seminole Canyon State Park, 8.5 km^2, occupies a very small part of the potential range of a hunter-gatherer group occupying the region. Nevertheless, data provided by the Seminole Canyon State Park study can be incorporated into a larger data set. The same holds true for the Amistad NRA, albeit on a much grander scale. The shoreline of Amistad NRA extends 869 km (540 miles), and even though the area covered by federal property is quite narrow, the boundary around the lake provides a large potential area within which to gather archeological data.

The sample of regional settlement-pattern data that can be collected from Amistad NRA has a drawback similar to that of the Seminole Canyon State Park — both are situated within the low and deep canyons of the region. Even the small upland areas of Amistad NRA are located close to deep canyons or tributaries. The potential exists, however, for survey data to provide critical new information regarding settlement patterns along the major streams and along the lower reaches of their canyon tributaries. As such, Amistad NRA represents a significant survey opportunity within the lower canyons on an east-west axis between the Devils and the Pecos rivers.

In order to provide an effective comparative sample, survey information must be collected in a manner that allows comparability among many data sets. For this reason, terminology should be standardized and clearly defined. Survey coverage should be accurately reported so that site density figures can be calculated and compared. Finally, the survey should provide the kind of data at a level of resolution that conforms to a well-defined research design and that will generate a meaningful outcome. Because the region consists of site types and feature types that represent redundant activities across the landscape, survey needs to be conducted beyond the level of establishing general site characteristics.

Effective surface survey has been conducted in this region that can provide meaningful data with which to infer subsistence/settlement patterns. Saunders (1992) demonstrated that distinctions in technological organization may be discernible across the landscape using surface survey data. The resolution of Saunders' data, however, is much higher than that of current survey methods in the Amistad NRA. In a survey of Hinds Ranch and Blue Hills, Saunders (1992) provided a very high-resolution, minimal definition for a site, and included data on isolated artifacts. He also collected data on tool types represented at small sites. Such a level of resolution is necessary in order to gain the data necessary to answer questions about technological organization, subsistence, and settlement patterns.

MANAGEMENT OBJECTIVES AND THE ASMIS DATABASE

Although specific management objectives varied among the SAIP and low-water surveys synthesized in this report, survey outcomes have been combined and incorporated within the ASMIS database by NPS personnel. Each survey recorded information about overall site condition good, fair, poor, or unknown. The database also contains information regarding disturbance levels (i.e., loss or displacement) incurred by the sites low, moderate, severe, or unknown. Sources of site impacts were also recorded; in most cases, sites are experiencing impacts from multiple sources. Assessing access to sites is an important part of a resource management plan since sites that are easily accessible to the public have a higher risk of being affected by looting or other impacts. Public access to sites has been evaluated on a qualitative scale that includes the categories of open, occasional, or undetermined.

The data potential of the sites has been evaluated by several different qualitative assessments. These include the amount of information a site could potentially yield, the overall integrity of site deposits, the overall condition of the site, the potential of the site to yield datable material, and the uniqueness of the site. In many cases, data potential cannot be accurately assessed by a reconnaissance-level survey, and the potential of many sites has yet to be determined.

The final category of site assessment addresses the issues of work accomplished and recommendations for future research. This category provides a progress report for cultural resources management at Amistad NRA. The work accomplished has been evaluated for most of the sites, and management or study recommendations have been determined for most sites in the database. These recommendations reflect the level of documentation and the type of documentation that has occurred at a site. Recommendations include suggestions such as conducting a literature search, mapping a site, performing a condition assessment, and evaluating a site.

SITE-BASED SURVEY:
SITES, ISOLATES, AND SITE TYPOLOGY

Site Definition, Site Boundaries, and Site Typology

Database applications and research designs demand a consistent means of identifying and characterizing archeological manifestations. For survey within Amistad NRA, a site-based approach has been adopted and carried out for several years. An archeological site is a discrete, bounded location where humans lived or worked and left behind physical evidence of such work that can be described in some manner by a researcher (Feder 1997:42). A consistent set of criteria that provide the minimal definition of a site allows data from different surveys to be compared. For this reason, I suggest using the following site definition, together with criteria that establish the minimal definition for a site. Both the site definition and the minimal criteria provided below are based on other field studies conducted in arid lands throughout the southwest including Saunders (1992); Sanchez (1999:39) and the current definition utilized by the Western Archaeological Conservation Center.

A site is any discrete locality containing potentially interpretable cultural material. Discrete refers to the fact that the material is spatially limited. By interpretable, it is meant that there are artifacts of sufficient quality or quantity to be able to make inferences about behavior at the locus. Cultural materials refer to artifacts, ecofacts, and features. *Minimally, a site is defined as a locus containing a least 10 artifacts and/or one feature within an area measuring 10 m².*

Although I have presented this definition as a suggested norm to which future site surveys may conform, no single site definition is applicable in all situations. For this reason the ultimate determination of a site remains the decision of the field or project director, who may need to change the definition to fit a specific context. For example, it is difficult to determine boundaries of quarry sites located in extensive surface gravel deposits commonly referred to as the Uvalde gravels. Determining whether flakes or core fragments resulted from human activity or natural fires may be impossible in this context, and the field director may decide to impose a more exacting definition of a site that includes formal tools or specific flake types, in order to make a site determination.

In many cases sites the archeologist must set the boundaries of sites that have discontinuous artifact distributions or unusual shapes such as a road or trail. The archeologist must then decide how to delimit the site and define its boundaries. The following suggestions are intended as a guide for field personnel making such decisions, and should not be taken as a rigid set of rules. The archeologist making the call should first and foremost be guided by common sense, and should clearly state reasons for the placement of site boundaries.

Generally speaking, if a discontinuous artifact distribution is observed in the field along a single landform type, the archaeologist may decide to lump a series of these artifact concentrations or features into a single site. This is often observed on alluvial terraces where several FCR features or chipped stone concentrations occur but are separated by gaps of a few to tens of meters. It is particularly appropriate to place several separate artifact concentrations into a single site if the discontinuity is obviously caused by erosional breaks in the same landform. On the other hand, if the artifact concentrations are separated by different landform types, such as an intervening canyon that interrupts a terrace, it may be appropriate to declare them to be two separate sites.

There are exceptions to the separate landform rule, however which are typified by many rockshelter sites, and by linear sites such as roads and trails. The talus of cultural debris emanating from many rockshelters often extends from the canyon wall to a point several meters across a terrace located below the shelter. In this case, the talus debris is clearly related to activity within the rockshelter, and should be included within the boundary of the site. Linear features (rock alignments, roads, trails) logically constitute a single site even though they may cross several landforms.

Defining the boundaries of linear features poses a special challenge. In many cases several separate trail or road segments are observable, and in this case it is up to the archeologist to decide if the segments are related to the same site before defining boundaries. In any case, linear features usually should be assigned the status of a single site only if they have observable and continuous lateral boundaries, and the archaeologist can make a reasonable argument that the separate segments are directly related to the same road or construction activity.

A site typology provides a useful means for categorizing and referencing sites for research and management purposes. It should be applicable not only to the park but also to the surrounding region; have a level of resolution appropriate to the quality of the available data; and it should be readily compatible with database applications. With these considerations in mind, the following site types have been adopted and applied to the survey database of 500 sites. Sixteen prehistoric site types are defined below for the Lower Pecos region. These types represent a slight expansion of prehistoric site typologies presented by Shafer (1982) and Bement (1989); however, the proposed typology is much simpler than other typologies that have been recently proposed for the park, which included up to 36 prehistoric site types. The definitions of historic site types are self evident and are listed below.

Assigning Site Types

The site typology presented in Tables 4.1 and 4.2 generally follows a convention that has been established in the region for 50 years (Bement 1989; Shafer 1988; Turpin 1995). To radically change this approach would only compound problems with integrating archeological studies conducted inside of the Amistad NRA with studies conducted elsewhere in the region. As a result, the 16 prehistoric site types represent a mix of site qualities. That is, some are defined by the landform upon which they are situated, such as sites located in rockshelters or overhangs. Other site types are defined by the most visible manifestation of cultural remains at the site, such as burned rock middens, lithic scatters, or hearths.

To reduce confusion, site types should be defined using a two-step process. First, it should be considered whether the site is sheltered or open. If it is a sheltered site, then it should be assigned to one of three types rockshelter, cave, or overhang. Second, if the site is open, then the site type should correspond to site content; i.e., the most abundant and dominant cultural remains present. Therefore, an open site with a massive accumulation of burned rock would be called a burned rock midden. An open site with a scatter of chipped stone would be assigned to a lithic scatter site type, and so forth. The total content of the site, whether it be sheltered or open, can be obtained by examining the feature table in the ASMIS database.

Historic site types and definitions conform to the primary industries which characterized the region over the last 150 years, namely ranches and railroads. By far, the majority of historic archeological sites in the region fit into one of these two general categories. Ranching refers primarily to historic Euro-American ranch operations in the late nineteenth or early twentieth centuries. Railroad sites date from the construction and operation of the railroad, primarily from 1880 through the early 1900s. Other than Native American pictographs that portray Spanish Conquistadors or cattle, sites associated with Spanish Colonial and Mexican settlements are not included in this database, but would be entered under the category "Historic — Hispanic."

Table 4.1. Prehistoric site types and definitions (adapted from Bement 1989; Black 1997; Labadie 1994; Shafer 1988, Michael Collins, personal communication 1999).

Alignment	Linear or circular arrangement of stones that usually does not exhibit the effects of heating; may occur in oblong stacks, paired stones in a continuous circle, or a circle of stones with a slab in the center; have been described as tipi rings, wickiup rings, or signal fires.
Burned rock midden	A feature consisting of fire-cracked rock, charcoal, darkened midden soils, artifacts, ecofacts, and often other associated or imbedded features.
Burial	Human or animal inhumation or cremation; may be primary or secondary.
Cairn	Ovoid or conical heap of stones built as a landmark or a monument; may be prehistoric or historic; prehistoric cairns may contain a burial.
Cave	A site located within a natural solution cavity in bedrock canyon or bluff walls; its depth is greater than its width.
Fire-cracked rock concentration	Amorphous concentration of fire-cracked rock in a discrete (sharply defined) area; often represents a disarticulated hearth.
Fire-cracked rock scatter	Low-density surface scatter of heat-altered or burned rock, with or without lithic artifacts, that contains more burned rock than lithic artifacts.
Hearth	A clast-defined feature, usually of fire-cracked rock, that is circular to oval in plan view and approximately .5 to 1.5 m in diameter.
Hearths – multiple	Groups of two or more intact hearths (clast defined and .5 to 1.5 m in diameter); usually accompanied by artifact and fire-cracked rock scatters.
Lithic scatter	Surface scatter of chipped stone or ground stone debris, including flakes, cores, early stage bifaces, etc., with no other features.
Midden	Consists of darker, organic-stained soil and increased concentrations of cultural remains, including artifacts, ecofacts, and features; often contains concentrations of mussel shell and remains of vertebrate fauna; associated features may include surface scatters of lithics and/or fire-cracked rocks, pits, and hearths; note that fire-cracked rock is not a dominant component of middens.
Overhang	A cavity in a canyon/bluff wall that has a back wall and an upper horizontal element that serves as a roof; overhangs lack well-defined side walls.
Pictograph/petro-glyph	Painted or pecked images on a boulder or bedrock.
Quarry	A locale with a concentration of abundant raw lithic materials, and sufficient chipped stone debris to indicate quarrying activities and stone tool production. Debris may include some or all of the following: tested cobbles, exhausted cores, primary, secondary, and tertiary interior flakes, biface blanks or preforms and failures, bifacial and unifacial tools, sequent flakes, and burins.
Rockshelter	A site located in a natural cavity in bedrock canyon or bluff walls. It has well-defined side walls and its width is greater than its depth.
Sinkhole	A concentration of cultural debris located in a depression in the land surface that opens into an underground passage or cavern that was formed by solution; burials are often identified in sinkhole sites.

Table 4.2. Historic site types and definitions (adapted from Labadie 1994; Mayberry 1997).

Dam	Water-control features built across a ravine or canyon to hold water for livestock
Historic Structures	A category for historic buildings that cannot be associated with either the railroad or ranching industry
Historic Trash Dump/Scatter	Discrete surface concentrations of historic trash
Historic - Miscellaneous	Historic sites that cannot be associated with either the railroad or ranching industry
Railroad - Miscellaneous	Includes all loci other than buildings that were associated with nineteenth-century railroads; may include ovens, walls, berms, tunnels, or the bed of the railroad
Railroad Structure	Historic structures, primarily coursed masonry, associated with the construction or operation of the railroad; many were built by businesses that existed when the railroad was constructed
Ranching - Miscellaneous	Includes facilities associated with ranching, such as fences, fence post alignments, or rock piles of various or unknown functions
Ranching - Nonresidential structure	Includes structures such as barns, corrals, or storage sheds
Ranching - Residential structure	Usually masonry/cement buildings associated with other ranching features
Trail/Road	Vehicle or pedestrian trails of historic age; e.g., U.S. Army trail known as Lieutenant Bullis' Trail that served as a crossing for the Pecos River

Two site types – a cairn and a trail/road – potentially represent either historic or prehistoric manifestations. Cairns are rocks arranged into a pile that may have served as a boundary marker, landmark for a border or canyon/river crossing, or to mark a burial location. Most burial cairns are prehistoric, but excavation of cairns is required to make a chronological determination. Trails and roads may be associated with the cattle industry, military activity, or may be Native American in origin. There are sites that may defy placement into any category. Nevertheless, adherence to the site typology will generate a usable database and allow for consistency between different survey efforts.

SURVEY METHODS

Park Boundaries

Any discussion of survey methods must first explain how the park's boundaries are defined. Amistad NRA has two boundaries – the "fee-simple boundary" and the "legislative boundary." The fee-simple boundary constitutes the current limits of federal ownership within the park, the area that has been purchased and is currently owned by the National Park Service. This boundary is defined as the canyon areas of the Rio Grande, the Pecos River, and the Devils River, up to the 1144.3-ft elevation contour, in most areas, and up to 1117 ft in a few areas.

The legislative boundary constitutes the maximum size to which federal ownership within the park may potentially expand. When Amistad NRA was created, the maximum allowable area of federal ownership was limited to 58,500 acres (Public Law 101-628; cited in Labadie 1994:Appendix C). Because the current area of federal ownership within Amistad NRA is 57,292 acres, the additional acreage constitutes an area that Congress has set aside as potential park land, but has not purchased. As such, the additional legislated area beyond the 57,292 acres remains in private ownership. Under current law, Amistad NRA is legally able to expand by 1,208 acres, pending the availability of funds.

The specific location of this additional acreage is limited to lands upstream of Seminole Canyon, extending up the Rio Grande to an area around Langtry, and proceeding northward along the Pecos River to the area around the railroad bridge which crosses the river just north of U. S. Highway 90. In this section of the reservoir, the legislative boundary is defined as the area above the 1144.3-ft contour up to the canyon rim. The boundary along the Rio Grande downstream of Seminole Canyon, and along the entire Devils River arm of the reservoir, is fixed at the 1144.3-ft contour. Figure 2.1 illustrates the approximate location of the park boundary relative to major streams, highways, towns, and railroads in the region. It would, however, require a very large scale map to distinguish between the legislative and fee-simple boundaries because in many cases they are located just a few hundred feet apart.

Survey Boundaries

Survey boundaries for the projects varied according to elevation parameters; i.e., above or below flood-pool elevation. SAIP goals were to document the extent of cultural resources on federal lands, and thus included all lands below 1144.3 ft in elevation. The BES project boundary was defined in the original task directive as "the immediate vicinity of the recreation area" (PL 101-628, Sec. 506, Sec. C; see Appendix A). As stated, upstream of Seminole Canyon, the survey boundary included all lands above the flood-pool elevation (1144.3 ft), but below the canyon rim. Included were all shorelines, river terraces, intervening side canyons, cliff faces, and associated uplands (Appendix A). This constitutes an area of approximately 8,000 acres that is not currently owned by NPS.

The BES objective was to identify prominent sites with high data potential that were threatened or imperiled and that could be acquired by donation or fee simple purchase for future management by NPS. Because the maximum expansion of Amistad NRA was limited to 1,208 acres, a set of criteria were necessary to rank the sites according to data potential and management prospects. These criteria included proximity of a given site to park ranger patrols, time required to access and monitor the site, and the site's potential for public interpretation (cf. Labadie 1994:29-30).

Field Methods

BES Field Methods. Field methods for the two surveys differed according to the stated goals of each project. The boundary-expansion surface survey, as dictated by PL101-628, was designed to locate sites within the generally defined zone of expansion – that is, between the canyon rim and the 1144.3-ft contour. Thus, the task directive for BES focused upon locating potential properties for park acquisition, rather than upon 100-percent survey coverage. No artifacts were systematically collected during BES from any identified properties. Instead, properties – primarily rockshelters – were located, revisited, and evaluated, with estimates made of the necessary acreage for purchase. BES did not evaluate sites for inclusion to the National Register of Historic Places (NRHP), but rather evaluated sites based upon a set of 15 criteria, including both research potential and management goals (see above). Although these are not typical evaluation standards for archeological resources, much of the data utilized to make these determinations have been entered into the current database. Based on BES results, 298 sites were positively evaluated for acquisition – 219 of these were considered high priority and 79 were considered low priority (Labadie 1994).

SAIP Field Methods. By contrast, SAIP was intended to be a standard archeological survey geared toward documenting and evaluating the cultural resources within the boundaries of Amistad NRA.

The general mandate of SAIP directed parks to describe and assess the status of archeological inventories and to establish strategies and goals for performing future archeological inventories (Aubry et al. 1992:17). The SAIP survey at Amistad NRA was conducted as a pedestrian-level survey; however, sites were not evaluated for inclusion to NRHP. A total of 398 sites was documented during SAIP, 350 of which were located on private property, but within the park's legislated boundary as defined by PL101-628.

Because there is no research design on file for SAIP, survey method details have been extracted from a draft report that essentially combined the results of both surveys, and from data on other sites located within Val Verde County (Mayberry 1997). The SAIP investigation consisted of a surface survey designed to record archeological holdings. Survey personnel were directed to cover 100 percent of the designated study areas (Mayberry 1997:V-2); however, in many areas coverage extended beyond 1144.3-ft in elevation, leading to problems with access to private lands. Most of the sites examined during BES were revisited and mapped, noting all visible features.

Although survey coverage was described in a draft report (Mayberry 1997), the total size of the areas that were surveyed area has not been reported, and USGS maps showing survey coverage were not included in documents submitted to TAMU. Four general areas within Amistad NRA were surveyed: (1) the eastern bank of the Devils River from the mouth of Rough Canyon to Satan Canyon; (2) the western bank of the Devils River from Castle Canyon to Slaughter Bend on the opposite bank from Satan Canyon; (3) the United States' side of the Rio Grande shoreline and associated tributary canyons from Box Canyon to the Pecos River; and (4) the United States' side of the Rio Grande shoreline on either side of Rattlesnake Canyon, including Rattlesnake Canyon and the adjacent uplands. Fieldwork resulted in a surveyed block along the east bank of the Pecos River from the Rio Grande to Deadman's Canyon and on the west bank of the Pecos from the Rio Grande to the apex of Nine Mile Bend. Survey coverage in other areas of Amistad NRA was broken into small, discontinuous plots.

Low-water Survey Field Methods. The following description of method is based on a document on file at the Amistad NRA (Appendix B). In response to successive years of drought, the International Boundary Water Commission (the governing agency responsible for regulating lake levels) lowered the lake as much as 52 ft below the reservoir pool level. As a result, numerous archeological sites were exposed for the first time in decades. The need arose to both inventory and monitor cultural resources within the drawdown zone, leading to the low-water archeological surveys of 1995, 1996, and 1997.

Because of the extensive size of the survey area (540 miles of shoreline), it was not possible to conduct a 100-percent survey during the low-water projects; instead, a subsample of the total shoreline was selected for survey. Previous survey results indicated that higher archeological potential was linked to certain landforms located within the park. High-priority survey areas were selected on the basis of two criteria: (1) the location of frequently visited areas; and (2) topographic areas with high archeological potential regardless of visitation levels. High-priority topographic areas, together with archeological expectations and other details of the low-water survey protocol, are provided in Appendix B, a draft survey model for the project.

The SAIP and the low-water surveys were identification-level studies that were not tasked with determining eligibility for the National Register of Historic Places. These were pedestrian reconnaissance studies that had the primary goal of determining the location, boundaries, size, and type of sites within the boundaries of Amistad NRA.

Chapter 5

SYSTEMWIDE ARCHEOLOGICAL
INVENTORY PROGRAM, 1991–1993, AND
LOW-WATER SURVEYS OF 1995, 1996, AND 1997

This chapter is based on a review of documents and data submitted to Texas A&M University (TAMU). As a result, much of the information has been interpreted from draft documents (e.g., Mayberry 1997; and Appendices A and B of this report), from archeological site data forms, and from unverified data files. The summary of the cultural resources inventory is based upon a sample of 500 sites contained in the Archeological Sites Management Information System (ASMIS) database for Amistad NRA. The ASMIS database itself is a work in progress, and the latest version was submitted to Texas A&M University on October 31, 1999.

The level of survey documentation has limited the detail of some material presented in this chapter. Survey coverage rates could not be determined because notes regarding personnel hours and area coverage were not part of the documentation submitted to TAMU. Survey area was computed using descriptions from a draft report by Mayberry (1997) and from tables included in the documentation submitted to TAMU. Survey area sizes should be considered general estimates.

Results of the BES-SAIP and low-water surveys are reported as separate investigations and presented in a summary fashion. Subsequently, results of SAIP were combined with the low-water survey results into a single database in order to provide a comprehensive impression of cultural resources within and adjacent to Amistad NRA.

SURVEY RESULTS

BES-SAIP 1991–1993 Survey

Survey coverage was distributed in a series of target areas along the three major drainages of the park (Figure 5.1). These parcels were located on the west and east sides of the Devils and Pecos rivers, and on the north side (United States' side) of the Rio Grande. Parcels surveyed along the Rio Grande were located between the Pecos and Devils rivers, and on the Rio Grande upstream from its confluence with the Pecos River.

A total of 398 archeological sites was documented during the BES and SAIP surveys, including 143 previously recorded sites and 256 new sites. Of these, 350 sites were located on private property within the legislated boundaries but adjacent to the Amistad NRA, and 49 were sites situated on federally owned properties at or below an elevation of 1144.3 feet above mean sea level. Since NPS personnel were barred from most privately owned sites after August 1992, 88 sites were not completely recorded.

Summary results of SAIP/BES investigations are presented in Table 5.1. Coverage was estimated from the text descriptions and maps contained in draft documents submitted to TAMU. Six survey areas were included in the SAIP/BES projects; combined, these investigations covered an estimated 5,979 acres

Table 5.1. Survey area coverage and site density from BES and SAIP investigations.

Survey Area	Site Count	Area Surveyed (km²)	Area Surveyed (acres)	Sites/km²	Sites/100 acres
Devils River Total	66	7.8	1927	8	3
Rio Grande Total	135	8.1	2001	17	7
Pecos River Total	197	8.3	2051	24	10
Total All Sites	**398**	**24.2**	**5979**	**16**	**7**

(24.2 km²). Because of difficulties documenting acreage in canyon areas, it is useful to translate this acreage into miles of shoreline covered in order to determine how much of Amistad NRA property was surveyed. The linear shoreline distance covered by the survey is estimated at 105 mi (169 km). This means that the survey covered about 19.5 percent of the 540-mile-long (869-km) shoreline of Amistad Reservoir. It targeted several parcels of land on the Devils River, the Rio Grande, and the Pecos River, with survey coverage fairly equally divided among the three major drainages. The Devils River survey covered 1,927 acres, the Rio Grande survey included 2,001 acres, and the Pecos River survey comprised 2,051 acres. With the exception of the Pecos River, which was surveyed almost continuously on both sides from its confluence with the Rio Grande to Nine Mile Bend, the survey was conducted in discontinuous parcels spread throughout the reservoir.

Results of the SAIP/BES investigations indicate that site density varies among the six survey areas, and from drainage to drainage (Table 5.1). A total of 66 sites was noted on the Devils River, 135 sites on the Rio Grande, and 197 sites on the Pecos River. Site density was highest on the Pecos River with 10 sites per 100 acres (24 sites/km²), and lowest on the Devils River with three sites per acre (eight sites/km²).

Twenty-two of the 256 newly recorded sites were located wholly or partially on Amistad NRA property, and 234 were located on private property but within the park's legislated boundary. Recall that the legislated boundary consists of property that remains in private hands but lies within the area legislated for acquisition. Many of the previously recorded sites had been mapped on older, 15' U.S.G.S. maps (1:48,000) and had to be relocated on the newer, 7.5' maps (1:24,000). In many cases, relocating and mapping sites was critical because the older maps and site locations proved to be inaccurate.

Low-water Surveys of 1995, 1996, and 1997. The low-water archeological surveys were designed to assess cultural resources within the drawdown zone that became visible due to lower water levels following an extended drought. The survey focused on the Devils River and the Rio Grande drainages (Figure 5.2). The 1995 survey was located on the Devils River above Rough Canyon, while the 1996 survey was located on the Devils River from the U.S. Highway 90 bridge to Rough Canyon. This area included San Pedro Canyon and Castle Canyon. The subsequent survey during 1997 covered the Devils River below the U.S. Highway 90 bridge and short segments of Rio Grande with associated tributaries, including Cow Creek and Rough Canyon (Figure 5.2). There are two canyons named Rough Canyon in the project area; one is a tributary of the Devils River, and one a tributary of the Rio Grande. The settlers of the region evidently ran out of descriptors for the remarkably rugged landscape.

The total area covered by the low-water surveys has been estimated from records and documents (Table 5.2). Survey coverage totaled 5,172 acres (20.9 km²), and total shoreline distance covered about 65.1 mi (104.5 km). The survey was primarily limited to landforms that had been previously submerged and to areas of the reservoir that were poorly documented prior to completion of Amistad Dam. The low-

Table 5.2. Total area coverage and site density from low-water surveys.

Survey Area (Year)	Site Count	Area Surveyed (km^2)	Area Surveyed (acres)	Sites/km^2	Sites/100 acres
Upper Devils River (1995)	15	2.7	678	6	2
Lower Devils River (1996)	67	5.0	1242	13	5
Rio Grande (1997)	20	13.2	3252	2	1
Total	102	20.9	5172	5	2

water surveys recorded a total of 102 archeological sites, all located on federal property within Amistad NRA, and all of these representing newly discovered sites.

Site density varied widely among the three areas surveyed (Table 5.2). For example, site density in the 1996 survey was five sites per 100 acres (13 sites/km^2), more than twice the density of two sites per 100 acres (six sites/km^2) recorded during the 1995 survey, and significantly greater than the 1997 survey conducted on the lower Rio Grande section of the reservoir with only one site per 100 acres (two sites/km^2). These differences in site density may be due to variable field methods, or it may actually reflect differences in site distribution. Although the variation in site densities cannot be explained yet, this discrepancy warrants further attention and should be the focus of future research efforts.

DATA SUMMARY OF CULTURAL RESOURCES IN THE ASMIS DATABASE

Data pertaining to the 398 sites recorded during the SAIP-BES 1992 1993 survey and to the 102 sites recorded during the low-water surveys have been combined for the current discussion. The database used to generate these tables was provided by the Amistad National Recreation Area and is part of the Archeological Sites Management Information System (ASMIS) system. ASMIS serves as the National Park Service's database for basic registration and management of prehistoric and historic archeological resources. It documents site location, site description, significance, condition, threats, and management requirements for known park archeological sites. The system provides a tool by which site information may be standardized and organized. ASMIS also provides the capability to assemble and report summary data needed for managing archeological resources within a park or group of parks.

This discussion is divided into three sections according to the organization of data in ASMIS. First, the archeological resources are reviewed in summary data format, including information on site size, components and temporal association, and site types. Second, management and administrative data are presented in summary form. These data include site condition, impacts, site access, and site evaluations. Finally, the overall status of the ASMIS database is reviewed in light of overall progress toward completion of a cultural resources assessment of Amistad NRA.

Cultural/Historical Data

Site Types. A summary of site types is presented in Table 5.3. A total of 14 prehistoric site types was identified during the two surveys, including 227 rockshelters, 92 burned rock middens, and 29 caves. These three site types accounted for 70 percent of all sites in the project database. In addition to these site types, 24 overhangs, 22 lithic scatters, 16 hearth sites, 25 fire-cracked rock (FCR) concentrations or scatters were documented, and 22 sites that fall into other categories. Although pictographs were located on 113 sites during the surveys, only three pictographs were assigned to the pictograph site type; the

Table 5.3. Site types recorded in the ASMIS database.

Site Type	Federal Jurisdiction	All Jurisdictions
Prehistoric Sites		
Alignment	1	4
Burned Rock Midden	71	92
Cairn	0	1
Cave	4	29
Fire-cracked Rock Concentration	4	6
Fire-cracked Rock Scatter	14	19
Hearth	4	8
Hearths, Multiple	7	8
Lithic Scatter	9	22
Midden	3	5
Overhang	2	24
Pictograph	0	3
Quarry	2	9
Rockshelter	20	227
Total Prehistoric Sites	**141**	**457**
Historic Sites		
Dam	0	5
Historic – Trash Scatter	0	9
Historic – Miscellaneous	0	1
Historic – Structure	0	1
Railroad	0	4
Railroad – Structure	0	3
Ranching – Miscellaneous	0	4
Ranching – Residential Structure	2	6
Ranching – Nonresidential Structure	0	1
Trail/Road	1	9
Total Historic Sites	**3**	**43**

remaining 110 were assigned feature status within the context of other site types. Sites were placed in the pictograph site type only if no other cultural materials were located that indicated an occupation. This points out the difficulty of assigning hunter-gatherer sites to specific categories, and illustrates why managers concerned with cultural resources need a database that can quickly access both site type categories and feature categories. The Amistad NRA database provides just that type of access.

In terms of site types, the two surveys yielded radical differences. For example, the SAIP/BES work accounted for about 98 percent of the rockshelters, but only about 40 percent of the burned rock middens. The low-water survey documented 14 of the 16 hearth sites reported in the database. This may be due to the fact that the low-water survey emphasized stream terraces recently exposed by falling reservoir levels where sites containing multiple hearths predominate. The SAIP/BES survey targeted canyon walls, rims, and adjacent uplands where rockshelters are typically located.

In all, 43 historic sites are reported in the database. Of these, seven are ranching sites with structures. Railroad sites are also noted at seven loci, including three railroad structures. Trails/roads are reported at nine different loci, with most of these related to ranching or railroad construction. Dam sites, most of which are probably associated with the ranching industry, were recorded in five locations. Eleven sites, most of them trash scatters, were not attributable to either the ranching or railroad industry.

Feature Types. The database presently contains 2,477 feature entries; of these, 2,380 are prehistoric and 97 are historic. The research design pointed out that hunter-gatherer sites often accumulate as the result of redundant activities at a single locus. As a result, hearths may be assigned as a site type when they are located in an isolated context, or as a feature type when they are noted either adjacent to or imbedded within a larger burned rock midden or rockshelter. Similarly, pictographs or burned rock middens are often reported as features within rockshelters or overhangs. Following Table 5.4, this discussion reviews the occurrence of the more prominent or abundant feature types, together with the site type contexts within which they appear.

Prehistoric Features. The reservoir area contains an abundance of three particularly important prehistoric feature types that require special protection and observation pictographs, petroglyphs, and burials. Pictograph features are recorded at 109 sites. As established in the database, pictograph features may refer to a solitary motif or to a large panel measuring several meters in length and height. Of the reported pictographs, nine are located in caves, 11 in overhangs, and 89 are located within rockshelter contexts. Petroglyph features are recorded at eight sites, all within rockshelters. All of the petroglyphs in the database are associated with pictograph features. In all, 22 burials located in 22 rockshelters or cave sites are noted in the database.

Most burned rock midden features are reported in association with open sites where they are categorized as burned rock midden sites. However, 11 are reported from caves, rockshelters, and overhangs. This number is most likely much higher, as most rockshelters with deep deposits have large burned rock midden accumulations imbedded within them.

A total of 71 individual or multiple hearth features is reported in the database. Most of the hearths are associated with open sites, either burned rock middens or sites that are composed of multiple hearths located on stream terraces. Thirty burned rock middens have associated hearths located around their periphery, and the majority of these have multiple hearths. Hearths are a common feature on stream terraces and are often found eroding from terraces that emerge as reservoir levels drop.

A total of 352 bedrock/boulder features has been recorded at 173 sites. Bedrock/boulder features include mortars, grinding facets, and cupules. These are not individual feature counts, but instead refer to occurrences of bedrock/boulder complexes. For example, each report of a mortar in the database may refer to a solitary mortar or dozens of mortars. Complexes containing mortars, grinding facets, cupules, and grooves are common in the region. Bedrock boulder features, commonly associated with rockshelters, have been reported at 124 rockshelter sites, but they may occur almost anywhere there is exposed bedrock. They have been reported with 10 different site types, including burned rock middens, caves, overhangs, FCR scatters, hearths, and stone alignments that occur on exposed bedrock along canyon rim areas. Bedrock features often occur with pictographs, and the database notes that mortars are present at 54 sites with pictographs.

Historic Features. Table 5.4 contains a summary count of selected historic features reported in the database. Historic features are primarily associated with nineteenth or early twentieth century ranching or railroad sites. Ranching features include standing structures, trails/roads, foundations, cisterns, watering troughs, windmills, machinery, walls, fences, dams, berms, trash scatters, and cairns. Railroad features include structures, baking ovens, railbeds, cairns, trash scatters, trails/roads, and rock alignments. Historic graffiti is reported from 22 sites spread across the entire reservoir area. Graffiti is associated with both the railroad and ranching in the region.

Table 5.4. Counts of selected prehistoric and historic feature types (from ASMIS database records).

Feature Type	Total Feature Count	Features on Federal Jurisdiction
Prehistoric Features		
Bedrock/boulder (mortar, cupule, facet, or groove)	352	53
Burned rock midden	126	9
Midden	183	15
Burial	22	4
Hearth (solitary or multiple)	71	51
Petroglyph	8	1
Pictograph	109	11
Historic Features		
Cairn	3	0
Cistern	3	1
Dam	5	0
Graffiti	22	2
Structure	29	0
Trail/road	11	0
Water trough	7	0

Site Size. The distribution of sites by size is presented in Table 5.5. Site size is extremely variable throughout the study area, ranging from a solitary hearth that measured 1 m^2 to a complex of burned rock middens that measured 1,344,600 m^2. The size of 37 sites remains unreported in the database.

The very broad range of site sizes affects descriptive statistics. For example, the mean site size for the 500 sites in the database is 15,064 m^2, but the median is much smaller at 350 m^2. Similarly, the mean size for sites identified during the SAIP survey is 17,032 m^2, but the median is smaller at 300 m^2. There is also a disparity between the mean size of sites recorded during the low-water surveys; the mean is 8,513 m^2, but the median is 1,350 m^2. In each case, the mean site size is raised by a few very large sites in the study area. Only 15 of the 500 sites in the database are larger than 100,000 m^2. The median site size provides a more reliable figure for quick comparisons of site sizes between the two surveys. The median size of sites in the low-water surveys (1,350 m^2) is over four times larger than the median for sites in the SAIP (300 m^2). This may be a result of the different objectives of each survey. SAIP investigations concentrated in areas of narrow canyons and upland sites adjacent to canyons, while the low-water surveys concentrated on alluvial/colluvial terraces and broader canyons/creeks in the eastern half of the study area. Sheltered sites such as rockshelters and overhangs were most common in the SAIP field effort, while the low-water surveys identified more open sites with burned rock middens. Open sites located on alluvial terraces tend to occupy much larger areas than rockshelter sites, which are located within a physically restricted area.

Table 5.5. Site size distribution data from SAIP and low-water surveys.

Site area (m^2)	Number of sites
unreported	37
0–100	110
100–500	146
500–1,000	54
1,001–2,000	41
2001–5000	34
5001–10000	21
10,001–20,000	16
20,001–50,000	17
50,001–100,000	9
100,001–200,000	9
200,001–500,000	3
500,001<	3
Total	**500**

Cultural/Temporal Affiliation. The ability to evaluate sites according to cultural/temporal affiliation is useful for both research and management goals. The ASMIS database provides two data fields where aspects of site temporal affiliation can be recorded. These are cultural history (CULTHIST) and time period (TIMEPER), and refer to general temporal categories. Of the 500 sites in the database, 156 sites have been assigned to one or more prehistoric time periods, 43 to historic time periods, and 301 are either "undetermined" or "undetermined Native American." Of the 156 sites assigned to a time period, 42 are multicomponent sites. Prehistoric components have been assigned to a chronological period primarily based upon the presence of time-sensitive artifacts. Many of the contexts are mixed, and many of the multicomponent sites are situated on stable surfaces, with little or no horizontal separation between the components. Very few of these evaluations are based on radiocarbon ages (Table 5.6).

Table 5.7 presents prehistoric site type totals by cultural affiliation. Cultural materials representing the Archaic period, particularly the Middle and Late Archaic periods, appear to be most abundant. This generally parallels results from other regional surveys (cf. Marmaduke 1978; Turpin 1982; Turpin and Davis 1993), but further work is clearly needed. The common assumption that the Late Prehistoric is poorly represented in the region is based on surveys that have concentrated on canyon areas. There is little survey evidence from upland areas away from the canyons. Further, the fact that cultural chronology remains undetermined for 301 of the 500 sites, roughly 80 percent, is a clear indication that more work needs to be accomplished at the sites which have been recorded. Many of these sites, especially lithic scatters and hearth sites or FCR concentrations and scatters, may be difficult to date.

Table 5.6. Cultural/historical components listed in the ASMIS database.

Cultural Affiliation	Number of Components
Euro-American	43
Late Prehistoric	20
Late Archaic	58
Middle Archaic	56
Early Archaic	14
Late Paleoindian	8
Undetermined or Undetermined Native American	301
Total	**500**

Table 5.7. Known prehistoric components by site type (42 sites contain multiple components).

Site Type	Archaic	Early Archaic	Middle Archaic	Late Archaic	Late Prehistoric
Burned rock midden	12	6	24	20	6
Cave	2	1	2	2	1
FCR scatter	2	0	2	4	0
Hearth (multiple or solitary)	2	1	3	3	1
Lithic scatter	2	0	4	4	0
Rockshelter	23	5	20	23	11

ADMINISTRATION AND ASSESSMENT INFORMATION

Results of both the SAIP/BES and the low-water surveys included management information that has been entered into ASMIS. Data from the fields pertaining to site management will be used to review site condition, impacts, site access, site evaluations where applicable, and the status of work accomplished at each site. In many cases, however, site recording efforts were restricted due to a variety of problems, including access to sites and limited funding. Much of the survey and evaluation efforts conducted under SAIP/BES were expended on privately held properties. In addition, the low-water surveys concentrated on sites in the drawdown zone of the reservoir, presenting a unique and complex set of challenges for archeological site management.

Jurisdiction

Because the goal of the BES was to identify properties for acquisition situated outside the boundaries of Amistad NRA, the database lists a large number of sites that are located on private property. An assessment of sites on private property has been published with the goal of setting priorities for future acquisition (Labadie 1994). There are 144 sites in the current Amistad NRA database that are located on federal property, five on state property, 343 on private property, and eight that are undetermined. Discussions of site management will distinguish between sites on Amistad NRA property and sites on private property. Although 15 of the 144 sites located on federal land extend into private property, for the purposes of this discussion they are placed under federal jurisdiction. Obviously these sites present a special problem for the manager, but the fact that they are at least partially located on federal property means they must be recorded and managed.

Site Condition

Although the SAIP/BES investigations and the low-water surveys evaluated sites in terms of overall condition, many were not evaluated according to ASMIS standards. Where applicable, these survey evaluations were included as data entries in ASMIS. What is known about the overall condition of sites, the level of damage to sites, the source of site damage, and the potential for future damage to sites is reviewed in this section.

According to the ASMIS database, of the 144 sites located wholly or partially on federal property, three are in good condition, four are in fair condition, and two are in poor condition (Table 5.8). The condition of the remaining sites has been entered as unknown because the assessments conducted in the field did not meet criteria stated in the ASMIS definitions. Likewise, of cultural resources on private or state property, the condition of 322 sites requires further evaluation. The primary sources of damage to sites in the region are summarized in Table 5.9. Most sites are currently affected by more than one

Table 5.8. General site-condition assessments according to jurisdiction.

Site Location[1]	Site Condition				
	Good	Fair	Poor	Unknown	Total
Federal Jurisdiction	3	4	2	135	144
Other or Undetermined Jurisdiction	9	8	9	322	348
Total	**12**	**12**	**11**	**457**	**492**

[1] Jurisdiction for eight sites is undetermined.

Table 5.9. Impacts affecting cultural resources according to jurisdiction.

Type of Impact	Federal	Other	Total
Erosion - general	42	222	264
Grazing/trampling - livestock	48	200	248
Vandalism	22	106	128
Rodent activities	13	114	127
Vegetation growth	18	71	89
Flooding or inundation	64	4	68
Erosion-water	34	18	52
Camping	21	8	29
Rock fall	1	27	28
Previous scientific research	6	19	25
Road or highway - construction/operation	14	8	22
Campfire building	10	9	19
Pest infestation	3	15	18
Unassessed	2	16	18
Unauthorized collecting	13	2	15
Animals	12	5	17
Theft or looting	4	6	10
Visitor use/visitation - general	9	1	10
Boating	6	1	7
Graffiti	0	4	4

type of impact. The most common problems are livestock trampling and erosion; other problems include vandalism, animal burrowing, vegetation growth, and flooding.

While the sources of damage to sites are well documented, the degree of damage to sites remains poorly understood. As noted in Table 5.10, the effect of impacts on sites within Amistad NRA boundaries is undetermined for 92 of the 144 sites in the database. Similarly, the overall level of threat to sites is poorly documented, as shown in Table 5.11. Of the 144 sites located wholly or partially on federal property, the level of threat for 121 sites is undetermined.

Table 5.10. Threat effect assessment for cultural resources according to jurisdiction.

Threat Effect	Federal Jurisdiction [1]	Private or State Jurisdiction [1]
Negligible	4	3
Partial loss - irretrievable	48	49
Partial Loss - repairable	0	2
Undetermined	92	294
Total	**144**	**348**

[1] Jurisdiction for eight sites is undetermined.

Table 5.11. Assessment of the site threat levels according to jurisdiction (from ASMIS database records).

Threat	Federal Jurisdiction [1]	Other Jurisdictions [1]
Low	10	13
Moderate	1	3
Severe	12	7
Undetermined	121	325
Total	**144**	**348**

[1] Jurisdiction for eight sites is undetermined.

Research or Interpretive Potential

Evaluating site data potential is a primary goal of cultural resource evaluation. In the Lower Pecos region, many archeological sites provide remarkably well-preserved cultural materials, including some of the most spectacular pictographs in North America. An accurate assessment of a site's data potential can guide management decisions regarding activities that can potentially and adversely impact a site. Table 5.12 reproduces database entries of the data potential of sites located in Amistad NRA and private properties. Of the 144 sites located on federal property, the data potential of 121 sites remains unevaluated.

Table 5.12. Evaluations of site data potential according to jurisdiction.

Data Potential	Federal Jurisdiction [1]	Other Jurisdictions
High	5	4
Medium	9	4
Low	9	9
Unevaluated	121	331
Total	**144**	**348**

[1] Jurisdiction for eight sites is undetermined.

Recommendations for Further Work

During the course of the surveys and as a result of survey outcomes, decisions were made regarding the need for further work at sites on and adjacent to Amistad NRA. These recommendations reflect the current status of archeological site management in the region (Table 5.13). Note that site condition assessments are needed for 124 of the 144 sites on Amistad NRA property. Literature searches have yet to be completed for 94 sites within federal boundaries, and site evaluations are needed for 32 sites. In general, the recommendations reflect a significant need for further evaluation of cultural resources located within the boundaries of Amistad NRA before further management recommendations can be made.

SUMMARY OF SAIP AND LOW-WATER SURVEYS

The BES and SAIP surveys began in December 1991 and continued through the end of April 1993. BES was intended to identify particularly important cultural resources on land within the park's legislated boundary, but situated on private property adjacent to Amistad NRA, with a view toward acquiring those properties with the highest data and interpretive potential (Labadie 1994). Although 219 sites were recommended as high priority for acquisition (Labadie 1994:22), funding has not been made available to move ahead with those plans. According to NPS documents, SAIP was designed to assess all cultural resources within park boundaries. Detailed scopes-of-work are not available for these surveys. The results of the two surveys have been treated as a single project, primarily because they were conducted within a continuous span of time and involved many of the same personnel.

The combined SAIP/BES projects covered approximately 5,979 acres (24.2 km^2) and 105 mi (169 km) of shoreline, or about 19.5 percent of the total Amistad Reservoir shoreline. A total of 398 sites was documented. Of the 256 new sites recorded in the survey, 22 were located on federal property. Overall site density within the SAIP/BES survey areas is estimated to be seven sites per 100 acres.

The low-water surveys were conducted to identify cultural resources that have emerged from the flood pool as reservoir levels dropped during an extended period of drought. These surveys were conducted during 1995, 1996, and 1997. Survey coverage totaled 5,172 acres (20.9 km^2) and identified 102 new sites. The low-water surveys covered an estimated distance of 65.1 mi (104.5 km). Site density varied among the three surveys, but averaged 5.4 sites per km or two sites per 100 acres. Differences in site density among the surveys are extreme, and it is very difficult to identify the reasons for these disparities. They may be a result of different field methods, errors in recording data, or may represent actual site distribution.

Table 5.13. Recommendations for further work at sites in the Amistad NRA according to jurisdiction (please note that many sites received recommendations for multiple tasks and column totals exceed the total number of sites).

Recommendation	Federal Jurisdiction	Other Jurisdictions
Confirm coordinates	26	52
Literature search	94	2
Map site	35	262
Reestablish location	3	0
Re-record	23	52
Site condition assessment	124	55
Site evaluation	32	265
Undetermined	4	65

The two major survey efforts covered an estimated total acreage of 11,151 acres. Because of difficulties measuring acreage within steep canyon areas, efforts to estimate total coverage of Amistad NRA property have been converted to linear shoreline distance. The SAIP/BES and low-water surveys covered an estimated total of 170 mi (274 km), or about 31.5 percent of the total reservoir shoreline of 540 mi.

Results of SAIP/BES and the low-water surveys were combined and the 500 sites were entered into the ASMIS database. All combined information has been presented in summary data format. Rockshelters (N=227) and burned rock middens (N=92) were the most common site types recorded. The 43 recorded Historic period site types included nineteenth and early twentieth century ranching and railroad construction loci.

The cultural-historical affiliation of prehistoric sites located within and adjacent to Amistad NRA is not well understood at this time. The time period is undetermined for 301 of the 500 sites in the database. As noted in the literature review, however, the region is dominated by Archaic period cultural resources.

A total of 2,477 features from the 500 sites was contained in the database. The most abundant of these are bedrock/boulder features that include mortars, cupules, and facets (N=352). In addition, a notable 109 pictographs, some panels measuring dozens of meters in length, have been recorded in the database. Historic features include structures, trails/roads, graffiti, and small water control dams.

According to the database, site condition assessments of 135 of the of 144 sites located within the boundaries of Amistad NRA are needed, an indication that the management status of most sites in the park remains in the beginning stage. Although threats to the sites have been identified and recorded, the overall effects of impacts have only been assessed for 52 of the sites in Amistad NRA (Table 5.10). Site data potential remains unevaluated for 121 of sites located in the park. In summary, management recommendations reflect the need for much more work at the vast majority of sites within the park.

Chapter 6

CONCLUSIONS AND RECOMMENDATIONS

Archeological surveys of Amistad NRA substantiate the richness of the prehistoric and historic resources in the region as well as the need for more work to complete the inventory of the park. The following general overview, drawn from survey documents and the GIS database, presents these resources in summary fashion. It demonstrates that Amistad NRA is located in an exceptional region for the archaeological study of foragers. The second section provides recommendations designed to help Amistad NRA obtain the best quality information to preserve and protect the cultural resources within its present and future boundaries.

OVERVIEW OF ARCHEOLOGICAL RESOURCES

The types of archaeological resources that are present on or adjacent to federal property exhibit clear distinctions most likely related to both the distribution of landforms in the region and to the history of land use in the region. This section presents a broad overview of the archeological resources in the region and their distribution within the park. It illustrates the predominant site types found in the park, and provides a general discussion of the potential that these sites have for providing archeological data or opportunities for interpretive presentations on the foraging lifeways of the Lower Pecos Archaic.

Rockshelters, Caves, and Overhangs

Throughout most of North America, rockshelters are a rare and unusual type of archeological site. In fact, Thomas (1988:167) refers to them as rare elements, sites that are seldom encountered in the archeological landscape. This is certainly not the case in the Lower Pecos region, where sheltered sites are remarkably common and diverse. Three types of sheltered sites identified in the current surveys are overhangs, rockshelters, and caves. Within or adjacent to Amistad NRA along the lower reaches of the Pecos River, the Devils River, and the adjacent Rio Grande, surveys have documented a total of 280 sheltered sites. Of these 280 sheltered sites, 26 are located within the current boundaries of Amistad NRA, and an additional 254 are located on property located within the legislated boundary of the park.

Sheltered sites were heavily utilized by foragers because they provided ideal residential/activity areas that were protected from the elements. The greatest single intrinsic value possessed by sheltered sites is their high potential to preserve artifacts and ecofacts that normally deteriorate when discarded in open contexts. For example, tools made of wood or fiber, human burials, clothing made of plant or animal material, and other perishable items are often recovered from sheltered sites.

The integrity of data sets provided by rockshelters is compromised by two major weaknesses. First, archeological deposits in rockshelters are often severely disturbed by human activities and animal burrowing because both are confined and focused by the natural limits of the shelter walls. Thus, the process of defining time/space relationships, critical to constructing archaeological chronologies, is often hampered by the condition of deposits in sheltered contexts, even though they are well preserved. Second, shelters, especially in the study area, are confined to the major drainages, so that the activities that occur within them provide very detailed accounts of foraging activities on only one part of the cultural landscape.

Despite these shortcomings, rockshelters contain almost every feature type in the study area and are rich in well-preserved material culture. The two most valuable feature types contained in sheltered sites are middens and pictographs. Most middens located in shelters measure dozens of cubic meters and contain desiccated plant fragments, bone, ash, fire-cracked rock (FCR), and other archaeological materials. Sheltered sites also provide an environment for the best preservation of rock paintings, which have been described as windows into the prehistoric cultures that left them (Boyd 1998b).

Of the 26 sheltered sites located on federal property, 20 are rockshelters, four are caves, and two are overhangs. Fourteen of the 26 sites contain midden deposits. Figure 6.1 shows the midden deposits in 41VV1380. In the center of the photograph is a boulder housing several mortars as depicted in the closeup in Figure 6.2. Many sites in the region contain archaeological deposits with well-preserved plant material in the same proximity as the fixtures and tools utilized for processing (Figure 6.3). These deposits represent an underutilized source of data for the study of foraging lifeways. Previous studies have utilized plant remains only for specific research purposes, such as ecological indicators (Dering 1979), dietary studies based on coprolites (desiccated human feces) (Bryant 1974; Sobolik 1991, 1996), and replicative experiments of agave and mesquite bean processing (Dering 1997, 1999). The fact that over 120 plant taxa have been identified from deposits in a single rockshelter (Dering 1999) is an indication that much remains to be learned regarding the foraging behavior of the region's inhabitants. Further, there has been only one comprehensive effort to study animal remains from archaeological sites in the region, and it was conducted at only one site (Lord 1984). Therefore, most of the data potential contained in rockshelters remains completely untapped.

As mentioned above, pictographs are among the most important archaeological resources of the Lower Pecos region. Sheltered sites within the park also contain spectacular rock paintings, as exemplified at 41VV187, Parida Cave (Figure 6.4). Of the 26 sheltered sites, 11 contain pictographs, many of which are spectacular panels measuring as much as 6 m in height and 50 m in length. Boyd (1998a, 1998b) has demonstrated the tremendous research potential contained in the rock paintings. Among the vast untapped potential of this database may be included the issue of forager territoriality as expressed by slight geographic variation in stylistic changes within the region (Boyd 1998b). This research is ongoing, providing evidence of the unique archaeological resources existing in the region.

Figure 6.5 depicts the distribution of sheltered sites, the majority of which are located along the Pecos River and along the Rio Grande near the confluence of these two rivers. This is primarily due to landform differences between the western and eastern ends of the park and the manner in which the reservoir filled the canyons of the three main streams. The steep, narrow canyons of the Pecos River contained far more rockshelters than the other rivers, and many of these sheltered sites are located above the floodpool. By contrast, the Devils River canyon walls were much lower prior to inundation, and any sites located along the lower reaches of that river remain under water. Upstream on the Devils River above Rough Canyon, however, there is a rise in the density of sheltered sites because the canyon walls are much higher and the sites are above the flood pool.

Despite the fact that some have criticized the overemphasis that archaeologists of the past have placed on rockshelters (e.g., Thomas 1986), the tremendous data potential that rockshelters contain for this region remains largely unrealized. Therefore, for the purposes of long-term management, the preservation of these sites should be paramount.

Pictographs and Petroglyphs

The Lower Pecos region houses spectacular examples of prehistoric art. Notable for their size and complexity, these polychrome and monochrome panels are very numerous. Few places in the world contain so many rock art sites within such a small area. In the current study alone, there are 109 sheltered sites with pictographs. Of these 109 sites with pictograph features, 11 are currently located within areas under federal jurisdiction. The other 98 sites are located within the legislated boundary of the park just beyond immediate federal jurisdiction.

The steep canyon walls and numerous sheltered sites provide an abundance of protected surfaces needed for the production and long-term preservation of the rock art. In addition, eight petroglyph sites have been noted. Although some descriptive work has been accomplished (Turpin and Bass 1997), petroglyph sites remain virtually unstudied, and relationships between petroglyph and pictograph sites in the region remain unknown.

As noted in Figure 6.6, most of the sites with pictograph features are located in the western half of the reservoir area, from Seminole Canyon upstream to Shumla Bend on the Pecos River. Another concentration of sites with pictographs is located along the Devils River near Satan Canyon.

Although the first objective should be to preserve these sites, the abundance of pictograph sites in the region presents great opportunities for research and outreach-oriented interpretive projects within the park. Rock art studies have not only provided insight, but have fueled research and debate regarding the belief systems and ritual practices of the Lower Pecos Archaic populations (Boyd 1996, 1998a, 1998b; Turpin 1990, 1994). However, data from rock art sites have scarcely been tapped. Boyd (1998b) has mentioned that a study of the geographic distribution of motifs in the region could illuminate issues of territoriality.

Burned Rock Middens

Burned rock middens are massive accumulations of debris, including fire-cracked rock, charcoal, and bone, that have accumulated from the use of earth ovens and other human activities. The photograph of 41VV1694 (Figure 6.7), a burned rock midden located on an alluvial terrace of the Devils River, provides an excellent example of the quantity of rock some of these middens contain. The surveys recorded a total of 92 burned rock middens, making them the second most common site type within the park. Most (N=71) of the burned rock middens noted in the surveys are located on federal lands; the remaining 21 are located within the legislated boundary of the park. In the current survey, examples of burned rock middens vary in size from 9 m^2 to 222,000 m^2.

Burned rock middens are also a very common feature type within sheltered sites. In addition to the 92 burned rock midden sites located in open contexts, there are 34 burned rock features located in rockshelters or caves. 41VV1694 and many of the burned rock middens described in the SAIP and low-water surveys were located on terraces of the Devils River or its tributary canyons (Figures 6.8 and 6.9).

Recent studies have revealed much about the structure and function of burned rock middens, yet the full range of activities occurring at these sites remains in debate (Black 1997; Dering 1999). Black (1997) has noted that burned rock midden sites often contain a wide range of features, and Dering (1999) has noted that burned rock middens in sheltered sites contain numerous plant taxa that are not directly related to processing in earth ovens or any other type of heating feature. That is, many residential activities occur in the immediate vicinity of burned rock middens, and these activities were not necessarily directly related to the large accumulations of FCR that characterize this site type.

Material remains in burned rock middens are not always temporally related to each other. Upland burned rock middens that are located on relatively stable landforms may contain the remains of cultural activities that occurred hundreds or even thousands of years apart. Compounding this issue is the fact that many earth ovens were successively used, new pits were dug adjacent to old pits, and rocks were frequently scavenged from previously utilized earth ovens (Black 1997). The debris from earth oven use seldom accumulates in a stratified manner, with older material on the bottom and newer material near the surface. Much mixing of old and new is observed throughout most of the area within a burned rock midden site.

Materials recovered from burned rock middens located on stable land surfaces are very difficult to temporally separate . This places a premium on the 47 burned rock middens that are located on surfaces that experience periodic deposition, such as stream terraces (Figure 6.8). Material remains from activities conducted on aggrading surfaces have a much greater potential to be horizontally separated by deposition of sediments resulting from periodic overbank flooding. Each level can then be related to a different time period, and any changes in the material culture are much more easily detected and described. Thus, recently discovered burned rock middens located along the Rio Grande, Devils River, and San Pedro Creek terraces may contribute valuable temporal data on regional foraging activities.

Hearths

As noted in Chapter 4, hearths are clast-defined (defined by rock fragments) features. They are usually composed of fire-cracked rock and are circular to oval in plan view, measuring approximately and .5 to 1.5 m in diameter. Groups of two or more intact hearths have been labeled multiple hearth sites, and are often referred to as hearth fields. Hearth fields are physical manifestations of campsites that were not occupied long enough or often enough to generate sufficient refuse to accumulate in a midden or a burned rock midden. There are 16 hearths or hearth fields identified in the current surveys.

Hearths may be located on non-aggrading or deflated surfaces or on alluvial terraces. Most of the solitary hearths or sites with multiple hearths (hearth fields) are identified on stream terraces (N=13) but they may also be located along canyon rims, interfluves, or other areas beyond canyon contexts. Hearths or hearth fields that are located on stable or deflated surfaces seldom have an abundance of material remains, especially biological remains (e.g., Dering 1998), but charred wood has been recovered and dated from hearths located on some stream terraces.

An excellent example of the data recovery potential from hearth features is provided by test excavations conducted in 1994 at 41VV1697 by Texas A&M University in conjunction with the National Park Service. As noted in Figure 6.9, this multicomponent site is located on the western terrace of the Devils River. It is located a few hundred meters downstream from 41VV1694, the burned rock midden illustrated in Figure 6.7. Test excavations noted a total of 24 hearths or disarticulated FCR scatters that were emerging from the falling pool levels of Amistad Reservoir (Figure 6.10). A Shumla dart point (Late Archaic), a Val Verde point (Middle Archaic), a possible Castroville point (Late Archaic), and a Perdiz point (Late Prehistoric) were recovered. It is likely that the erosion from falling lake waters may have caused the concentration of these diverse point types on the site surface. Three metate fragments and several manos were also noted at the site. The possibility that 41VV1697 is a stratified site was noted when a buried feature (Feature 13) was located in Test Unit 2. Flotation samples yielded littleleaf walnut fragments, acorn fragments, goosefoot seed, strawberry cactus seed, purslane seed, juniper seed, and six wood types (Dering 1995). This two-day mapping and testing project demonstrates the potential for data recovery within a hearth field located on an alluvial terrace, especially if the fields contain buried features. Most significantly, this site had been inundated by Amistad Reservoir for years, demonstrating that ecofacts and biological remains may be preserved under lake waters.

Quarries

Quarries are locales that provide raw material for the manufacturing of chipped stone tools. A total of nine quarries have been recorded in the current surveys. All of these locations are located in open contexts (Figure 6.11). Although quarries can provide insight into stone tool manufacture through the study of reduction processes, they are located on non-aggrading surfaces, making the study of technological change difficult because of the lack of temporal control.

Middens

Midden sites are accumulations of cultural debris manifested as organic-stained soils and increased concentrations of artifacts, ecofacts, and features. They are often rich in discarded mussel shell, animal bones, charred plant material, ground stone ,and chipped stone artifacts and debris. Middens are usually an indication of superior preservation and often have been quickly buried in alluvial or colluvial contexts. Most of the middens are situated within the San Pedro Creek area (Figure 6.12). All five midden sites noted during the current surveys are located on stream terraces.

Other Sites

Other site types located within the study area include alignments, lithic scatters, and FCR concentrations and scatters. Alignments are circular or linear arrangements of stones that may occur in stacks, paired stones in a continuous circle, or a circle of stones with a center slab. Although these are obviously of human origin, their exact function is difficult to determine. Some alignments in the Lower Pecos region, such as Infierno Camp (41VV446), are extensive and obviously constitute the remains of structural elements associated with a residential site, perhaps tipi rings. The alignments located and described within park boundaries are limited in nature.

Lithic scatters are commonly encountered on deflated or non-aggrading surfaces. Detailed recording and analyses of these small sites in a regional survey can elucidate information on technological organization on the landscape (Saunders 1992). However, the data potential of a single surface lithic scatter is low, and these sites are seldom studied in reconnaissance level surveys.

Fire-cracked rock concentrations or scatters are usually composed of disarticulated hearths or burned rock middens. Because these sites are commonly located on eroding surfaces, they are quite common on stream terraces, especially those emerging from the falling reservoir waters. Most of these sites have recently been noted along the Devils River and San Pedro Creek. The data potential for most FCR concentrations or scatters is probably low, but recording these sites should assist in understanding land use throughout the region, often leading to the discovery of intact features or deposits nearby. This was certainly observed during testing at 41VV1697, a site located on the Devils River terrace.

Historic Sites

In total, 43 historic sites are noted in the current project. Historic sites in the region consist primarily of the remains of nineteenth or early twentieth century ranching efforts, or the remains of the nineteenth century construction of the Southern Pacific railroad (Labadie 1994; Skiles 1996). Of these 43 sites, three are located on federal property and the rest are located within the legislated boundary of the park. The three sites located on federal property include two ranching structures and a trail, 41VV1428, that was constructed in 1875 by the U.S. Army. Known as Lt. Bullis' trail (Figure 6.13), it once crossed the Pecos River just north of the Rio Grande at the old low-water U.S. Highway 90 bridge, an area that was an old Indian ford on the river (Dolman 1995:42).

RECOMMENDATIONS

At the beginning of this project, examination of the database indicated that a different site typology was used during the SAIP survey of 1992 1993 than was used during subsequent surveys. Because the site typology used during SAIP was not compatible with others in the region, considerable effort has been expended to simplify the typology and bring it into accord with other regional site designators, and to reenter the site data. Also, in some cases, as between the BES/SAIP and the low-water surveys, field research protocols were not explicitly stated or consistent from one project to the next. This final section will provide recommendations for additional research, for field and recording methods, and for the kinds of investigations needed to aid future resource management efforts.

Recommendations are divided into three categories and are discussed in order of priority. The first part addresses the need for the park to establish a consistent set of protocols for field recording and cultural resource inventory purposes. Second, general areas within the park requiring additional survey are noted, and data needs within the existing cultural resource inventory are presented. The third and lowest priority discussed in this chapter presents an overview of data that would assist in achieving long-term research goals.

Field Protocol

Field Survey Methods. A field protocol detailing survey methods was not included in documentation submitted to TAMU for the SAIP. The field protocol should include the minimal definition of a site, which is furnished herein for future surveys (see Chapter 3). Reports also should include consistent records of survey transect widths. This information was provided in other regional surveys by Saunders (1992) and Turpin (1982). Both site definitions (see Chapter 3) and survey transect widths have been shown to affect site density calculations (Thoms 1988). A consistent protocol for recording tool types and feature types noted at sites needs to be established (cf. Saunders 1992). Therefore, determining and recording survey methods in a field protocol prior to a survey project will provide both a guide to the field crew and a frame of reference for other researchers attempting to interpret survey data.

Site Recording Forms. Field recording procedures should be designed to interface easily with the State of Texas Archeological Site Data Form, with ASMIS database fields, and with the local needs of the park. The current Amistad NRA site recording form meets many of these needs, but was developed before ASMIS was instituted in the park. Specifically, it lacks entries for much of the management information and some of the archeological/environmental data requested both on the State of Texas form and in the ASMIS database fields. It would be very useful to redesign the form to incorporate the categories on the State of Texas form and on the ASMIS site recording form (Davis et al. 1995:III, 1-7). Because a State of Texas Archeological Site Data Form and an ASMIS site recording form may need to be completed for each site, an alternative would be to use those two forms and design a small supplementary form to meet specific park needs.

Data Needs in the Current Site Inventory

At this time, Amistad NRA lacks detailed cultural/chronological and assessment information in its ASMIS database for many sites located within its boundary. As noted in Table 5.13, several management and data categories are in need of more work and will require return visits to sites. This table was adopted from the Study Recommendation entry in the Assessment Section of ASMIS. Recommendations include a site condition assessment, which is needed for 124 of the 144 sites listed in the database as being located within federal jurisdiction. Second, the data potential has not been determined for 121 of the 144 sites located either wholly or partly within federal jurisdiction lands (Table 5.12)..

Cultural Affiliation/Components. Identifying the components represented at sites and identifying multicomponent sites needs to be addressed in future research. In some cases it may be possible to glean information from the site report forms and place these data into the ASMIS database. Of the 500 sites in the current sample, 301 are listed as undetermined (see Chapter 5, Table 5.6).

Site Condition. The condition of each site should be assessed in the field by a professional archeologist. Site report notes often do not contain sufficient detail for a proper condition assessment. The criteria for recording site condition assessments should be built into the site report form in accordance with NPS policy. Condition assessments are listed as good, fair, poor, destroyed, or unknown, and must be accompanied by a condition assessment date (Davis et al. 1995:IV:140).

Site Data Potential. Data potential refers to the ability of a site to provide information important to understanding the prehistory or history of an area or region. It is synonymous with *archeological interest* as used in the Archaeological Resources Protection Act of 1979 and NPS regulations, and/or the language provided in the National Register Criterion D. Data potential of a site can change over time, becoming either more important or less important, due to many factors such as natural deterioration, vandalism or looting, reevaluation, advances in research technologies, or changes in research goals (Davis et al. 1995:131).

Locally Defined Fields. Currently there are two locally defined tables in the ASMIS database. One table identifies the person who described each archeological site in the database (Local 1), and another table provides the elevation of each site (Local 2). Two other very useful locally defined fields would include one that provides details of the pictograph/petroglyph sites in the region, and one that lists the specific landform information for each site. These entries could be built into the site recording forms.

Database Entry and Management. All databases require constant updating and verification. No matter how rigorous the data entry system, mistakes can be made. Data requirements change and often need adjustment of entries or fields within a database. Data needs are best determined by the park archeologist, as are data entries. Many categories in the ASMIS database do not exactly match information on site forms. This has happened because the categories on the site recording forms do not match the categories delineated in the ASMIS system. In addition, there were inconsistencies in the site recording forms due to a lack of a clearly defined field protocol. Because of these issues, it is recommended that a system of verification be instituted between Amistad NRA staff and the ASMIS System Administrator at WACC. Ideally, ASMIS entries would be closely monitored by the Amistad NRA park archeologist because the park archeologist has the most intimate understanding of sites within the park.

Additional Fieldwork

Based on results of the SAIP surveys, approximately 31.5 percent of the 540-mile reservoir shoreline has been surveyed, leaving almost 70 percent of the shoreline to be covered. General areas of the shoreline which need to be surveyed include the following:

Rio Grande:
(1) Along Zuberbueler Bend;
(2) From Rough Canyon to Cow Creek;
(3) Downstream from Cow Creek to near the confluence of the Devils River; and

(4) From Pump Canyon to Rattlesnake Canyon, and from Rattlesnake Canyon upstream to the limits of the Amistad NRA boundary.

Pecos River:
(1) The eastern side of the Pecos River upstream from Deadmans Canyon; and
(2) The western side upstream from Nine-Mile Bend.

GENERAL RECOMMENDATIONS FOR FUTURE RESEARCH

There is a need for large-scale, well-designed, intensive survey both within and without the park as NPS funding allows. The task of survey in this site-rich region remains largely incomplete, even though almost 2,000 sites have been reported from Val Verde County. The BES/SAIP and low-water surveys combined have covered approximately 31.5 percent of the park. Although park-sponsored field work covering much smaller parcels has been completed, less than 40 percent of the park has been surveyed for cultural resources.

Amistad NRA now has the necessary GIS software linked to the ASMIS database, allowing survey data to be compiled and analyzed on a regional scale. In particular, smaller low-density sites (e.g., Saunders 1992) that provide a more comprehensive view of land use are missing from the data set. This is a function of the presence of spectacular rockshelter and rock art sites, and the resultant emphasis upon these more conspicuous sites. A sample of specific areas within the park that include small sites or isolates, or a survey that adopts a nonsite approach would provide the data needed to establish a more accurate impression of land use in the park (cf. Saunders 1992). Details of recording methods have been reported in Saunders (1986, 1992).

Looking beyond the initial establishment of a cultural resources inventory, complementary data sets should be developed to support the survey data. Surface survey will eventually need to be supplemented with subsurface testing, particularly in areas that have the potential to yield stratified deposits in alluvial or colluvial contexts (cf. Thomas 1988:169). With the exception of the early Texas Archeological Survey Program survey and a few very small efforts within the park, none of the previously summarized surveys (e.g., Anderson 1974; Turpin 1982; Turpin and Davis 1993) mention subsurface testing, even though many of the sites within Amistad NRA are located on colluvial or alluvial terraces with a potential for buried cultural materials. Stratified sites located on alluvial terraces would provide important chronological data for the region. In addition, sites located in upland areas outside of canyons have not been tested (Anderson 1974).

Geoarcheological studies are needed in order to determine the kinds and distribution of landforms within the park. In the survey model for the low-water surveys (Appendix B), the statement is made that the distribution of sites is linked to landform. For example, the prediction is made that large fire-cracked rock features are more likely to occur on colluvial terraces adjacent to the confluence of main river channels and intervening side canyons than along any other portion of the side canyons. In addition, it is predicted that the greater the distance away from canyon rims, the lower the probability for surface lithic scatters. Another prediction is that certain pictograph styles (i.e., Red Monochrome) usually occur in the same topographic setting. So, the archaeological potential for a given area is linked to the pre-inundation topographic setting.

Efforts in the current project to incorporate landform data into the database were hindered by irregular recording of landform information in the site forms. A distinction is seldom made between a colluvial or alluvial terrace, and in many cases, the exact landform was not recorded. This is probably due, at least in part, to three factors. First, the use of volunteer labor in many of the surveys limits the accuracy of observations. Second, there is no specific section in the site survey form that addresses the category of landform. And third, the geomorphology of the vast majority of the park has not been studied, which means that the determination of landform needs to be made by someone who is very experienced in archeological survey and recognition of landscape features. The lack of comprehensive geomorphological study constitutes a major data deficiency for the study of archeological site distribution in the region. Pending comprehensive study of the geomorphology of the park, a very clearly delineated set of choices should be presented on the site form under a separate category entitled "Landform" so that the reporting of landform may be as consistent as possible. A consistent landform typology that is clearly defined and applicable to a field situation will allow survey crews to accurately and uniformly characterize the type of landform upon which a site is situated.

Data Needs and Future Survey

A brief review of some data needs for the region may assist the formulation of research designs for future survey in the region. Surveys that are geared to establish cultural resource inventories might not produce the data needed to solve these data deficiencies, but they can provide the researcher with the information they need to find sites with the potential to produce the necessary data. Given the tremendous potential exhibited by the cultural resources in the area, there are five research categories in which the data are notably deficient paleoenvironment, subsistence, cultural interaction, settlement patterns, and chronology.

Paleoenvironmental Domain. As previously explained, our understanding of paloenvironment in southern, central, and western Texas remains somewhat superficial and contradictory. The Lower Pecos region lies literally at the crossroads of the Trans Pecos, Edwards Plateau, and southern Texas Plains regions, and may provide evidence that allows several regional climatic records to be assimilated. There is considerable evidence of human occupation from 10,000 B.P. to present, and some of these deposits will eventually provide adequate data for environmental reconstruction (Bryant 1969; Bryant and Holloway 1985; Dering 1979). Although rockshelters contain detailed vegetation records, they may not be the most desirable for environmental reconstruction because of human selection and the fact that canyons are effective refugia for mesic plants. Thus, plant assemblages from archeological sites would be skewed by human selection and by the sheltering effects of canyon environments. On the other hand, alluvial terraces contain geomorphological records that provide regional signatures with potentially great time depth and a finer resolution than other deposits. Although the two most promising terraces, located at the confluence of the Devils River and the Rio Grande, and the Pecos River and the Rio Grande, are submerged beneath the waters of the Amistad Reservoir, there are promising terraces located on the Rio Grande just below Amistad Dam and along the Devils River at the current limits of the reservoir waters. Efforts should be made to survey these areas and to identify the alluvial terraces with the potential to contain cultural deposits with the longest time sequences.

Subsistence Domain. Despite the wealth of subsistence data available for the Lower Pecos, the vast potential that these cultural resources possess has not been adequately explored. Virtually all the data are based on coprolite studies from a two rockshelters, Hinds Cave, located near the Pecos River, and Baker Cave on the Devils River (Heubner 1991; Sobolik 1991, 1996; Williams-Dean 1978) . Although no macrobotanical studies of rockshelter deposits have been completed, a preliminary archaeobotanical study of Hinds Cave deposits has identified 121 plant taxa (Dering 1996), a testimony to the richness of the ethnobotanical record available in these settings. There is only one complete faunal study for the region (Lord 1978). Most of the coprolite studies have emphasized pollen, while other microfossils and macrofossils remain understudied. Data from shelters located on the Devils River, a much more mesic environment, are completely lacking. Subsistence data from open sites are completely lacking for the area.

Over the last ten years, only eight flotation samples, all from small FCR features located at 41VV1697 on the Devils River (Dering 1995), have been analyzed from the Lower Pecos, evidence of the lack of excavation that has been conducted in the region. Sites with great potential to yield subsistence data include burned rock middens, rockshelters, caves, and sites containing multiple hearths. There is a need to locate and characterize both open sites with potential to yield subsistence data, and sheltered sites that still contain relatively undisturbed deposits.

Settlement Patterns Domain. Archeological survey has the potential to contribute directly to this research domain. Within the context of hunter-gatherer research, settlement patterns refer primarily to the patterning of group mobility as reflected in the distribution of sites across the landscape (Binford 1980; Kelly 1995). In most cases, it is characterized as a seasonal round or as the movement of a group within its home range or territory. How often did groups move, where did they move, and why did they move? Within the Lower Pecos, this subject has been addressed by several authors, none of whom had access to adequate archeological survey data (Dering 1999; Marmaduke 1978; Shafer 1986; Sobolik 1996; Turpin 1995). The potential for combining good survey data with the remarkable preservation encountered both within rockshelters and in some of the open sites has yet to be realized. As discussed in Chapter 4, a good survey database is desperately needed that covers a large geographic area, and the data generated by survey within the boundaries Amistad NRA can provide an excellent start for such a database. Fine-grained survey that focuses on technological organization (Saunders 1992) can be combined with much larger reconnaissance-level surveys, such as the BES/SAIP and low-water surveys, contributing a geographic context to the debates over settlement patterns. This will be particularly effective now that the GIS database has been established for the park.

Cultural Interaction Domain. This research domain includes reconstructions of hunter gatherer social structure, social interactions, and belief systems. An area with such remarkable preservation of a wide variety of artifact types normally absent from sites has a tremendous potential for generating information regarding social structure, cultural interaction, and belief systems. Studies of pictographs (Boyd 1996; Turpin 1994), burials (Turpin 1988), and rockshelters (Shafer 1986) have demonstrated the region's data potential for the reconstruction of relatively intangible aspects of hunter-gatherer lifeways, including social structure, organization of living space, and belief systems. Turpin (1995:549), for example, has interpreted the Red Linear pictograph style as evidence for an intrusive Plains culture that moved into the area following buffalo herds. She argues for a similar intrusion during the Late Prehistoric period based on changes in weaving techniques, the introduction of cremation, and pictograph styles (Turpin 1995:550). Pictographs have a unusually high potential for reconstructing prehistoric belief systems and territoriality (Boyd 1998). A well-designed study that targets and properly records the distribution of pictograph motifs across the region has the potential to produce excellent data for the study of both belief systems and territoriality. The database is sufficiently rich that all of studies completed to date barely tap into the tremendous data potential in the region.

Chronometric Domain. The Lower Pecos region does not lack radiocarbon ages, as illustrated by Turpin's (1991) review of chronology for the region. Turpin (1991) reports on over 200 dates from the region, but the problem lies in the fact that the vast majority of these radiocarbon assays were completed in the 1960s and 1970s, most of the dates have excessively broad error ranges, and most of the dates were generated before carbon isotope ratios were considered standard procedure for evaluating dates. Because the botanical assemblages from these sites are rich in CAM plants (Dering 1999), these dates are somewhat problematic. Most of the radiocarbon assays come from rockshelter contexts. The stratigraphic contexts of many shelters are not published in great detail, and many are somewhat problematic due to the complexity of deposits. Although Turpin (1991:28) is able to generate a comprehensive chronological sequence for the region, the study reports many mixed strata within rockshelter deposits. Further, Turpin

(1991:25, 31) specifically identifies time periods within the Late Paleoindian and the Late Archaic periods that need refinement in the chronological sequence.

There is a great need in the region for a new suite of radiocarbon assays using current technology. Although this need cannot be addressed by archeological survey, future field work should target areas of the park that will most likely produce sites needed to solve chronometric issues. The problem posed by mixed deposits in rockshelters is best overcome by generating data from sites in alluvial contexts that contain deep stratified deposits. Because the most obvious sites in this category   Arenosa Shelter and the Devils Mouth Site   lie under Amistad Reservoir, this places a premium on all archaeological sites located on alluvial terraces within the park. The most likely area for finding sites of this type is located on the northern side of the Rio Grande just below Amistad Dam. This area should be considered to have cultural resources with extremely high data potential and should be surveyed as soon as possible. Another area of reasonably high potential is located on the Devils River just upstream from the highest levels of the reservoir, particularly within intervening side canyons where overbank deposits have left small terraces.

Evaluating Research Potential

This chapter provides an excellent opportunity to address the research potential of sites within the park, and to identify those properties most likely to generate data needed to satisfy the regional data deficiencies. In the Lower Pecos region, where archeological sites are so common, what attributes make a site valuable for research or interpretation? What sites most likely will not produce useful information?

The surveys summarized in this volume have provided the framework for a fairly comprehensive, although incomplete, cultural resource inventory. This constitutes a necessary step toward establishing a comprehensive historic context for the park. The previous research has generated evidence of human occupation spanning over 10,000 years, from early Holocene habitation sites to the ranching and railroad sites of the Historic period. Within this broad temporal span, surveys have defined archeological sites included within and adjacent to park boundaries, and have recorded their location. The site and feature typology established in this study will allow successive survey projects to generate comparable data, permitting continued expansion of the current cultural resource inventory. The site typology also provides an excellent means of providing a preliminary assessment of the type and quality of data it may contain.

There are several types of sites which may have a narrowly defined research potential applicable to only specific types of research designs, such as in the study of technological organization by Saunders (1992) which is discussed in Chapter 3. These include lithic and FCR scatters, FCR concentrations, bedrock features without associated features or deposits, and many quarry areas. Many lithic or FCR scatters/concentrations are remnants of sites that have been severely damaged by erosion or other disturbances. They are located in secondary contexts and often lack subsurface deposits and any diagnostic artifacts. Despite inherent limitations, these sites can provide important data for land use studies that require a thorough understanding of the regional distribution of all site types.

In the Lower Pecos certain unusual and rare site types have a very high data potential. These include all pictograph and petroglyph sites. Even severely damaged pictograph sites have the potential to yield important data, because only severely damaged pictographs, or paint fragments that are spalling off canyon walls, can be dated without compromising the integrity of a pictograph panel. Radiocarbon dates generated from the organic fraction of paint is a new and very promising development, and has recently been used to provide direct dates of the Pecos River Style and Red Monochrome art in the region (Hyman and Rowe 1997).

Rockshelters, caves, overhangs, or sinkholes that contain pictographs/petroglyphs, dry deposits, or burials are other unusual site types that have high research potential. Although rockshelters and caves with dry midden deposits are common in the Lower Pecos, there are very few regions in the world where this type of site exists. The kinds of data and the volume of data potentially recoverable from dry deposits has never been fully realized from these shelters. Excellent studies of perishable remains have been conducted, including surveys of basketry (McGregor 1992) and sandals and cordage (Andrews and Adovasio 1980). These studies provide a comprehensive view of artifacts seldom recovered from archeological sites, but amazingly no synthesis of subsistence or lifeways in the region has emerged. In addition, there is an increasing potential for the application of new technologies to the study of perishable archeological assemblages that are so abundant in this region. For example, a recent study examined sequenced DNA in desiccated botanical remains recovered from rockshelters in the region. This data contributed to a study of the evolutionary history of the plant genus *Yucca* L. (Clary 1997).

Burned rock midden sites located in open contexts constitute an understudied site type along the southwestern and western reaches of the Edwards Plateau. These sites represent accumulated debris from earth oven processing and other activities, and as such have a high potential to provide carbonized plant remains and other data pertaining to subsistence activities. Burned rock midden sites should be considered to have a high data potential if they contain subsurface deposits and if the fine fraction remains. Some burned rock middens, however, may have a greatly diminished data potential because of erosion from rising and falling lake levels. In many cases, burned rock middens located within a reservoir drawdown zone have been subjected to wave action that has completely removed the fine fraction, leaving only an accumulation of larger fire-cracked rock. Although the larger rocks from these sites remain in place, they may have little data potential beyond a general site distribution study.

Hearths or multiple hearth sites may be considered to have a very good research potential if they contain datable materials, sufficient ecofacts for faunal and botanical analysis, or diagnostic artifacts. These sites are less intensively occupied than burned rock midden sites and may contain information on a range of subsistence activities, including plant and animal procurement and processing. Because some of these sites probably represent single-use events, it may be easier in some cases, with good preservation, to identify and describe specific subsistence activities than at burned rock midden sites where multiple activities occurred at the same locus over a much longer time period.

Burials are usually located within rockshelters or sinkholes but may be encountered in open contexts. All burials require special consideration in a management plan. Cairns, which are large heaps of stones erected as a monument or landmark, may contain burials or artifacts. Cairn excavations in the region have yielded artifacts but no direct evidence of burials (Turpin 1982). However, cairns from other areas in western Texas and northern Mexico have yielded both inhumations (human remains that have not been cremated) and artifact caches (Mallouf 1987). Cairns have a high potential to contain either burial or artifact caches and should be considered to have a high data potential. All cairns containing human remains and other burial goods are subject to regulations governed by the Native American Graves Protection and Repatriation Act (NAGPRA).

There is a rich history of railroad construction and ranching in the study region (Labadie 1994). Historic sites relating to nineteenth or early twentieth century railroads and ranches have the greatest research potential, especially if they contain structures and diagnostic artifacts. Some sites, such at Lieutenant Bullis' trail, are associated with specific historic events. Dams identified in the region present a glimpse of ranching efforts to retain water in the areas between canyons before drilling equipment was effective and cheap enough to allow ranchers to drill wells through 600 to 800 feet of limestone bedrock. Railroad track beds, camps, and trash scatters have provided a rich assemblage of artifacts for the interpretation of life during construction of the southern intercontinental railroad. These sites are quite unusual and most probably have a high data potential.

Finally, the location or landform type upon which a site is located may be an important factor in assessing its research potential. Chronometric issues are best addressed by data obtained from sites with deep, stratified deposits. In the Lower Pecos region, these sites are located on alluvial terraces (Dibble 1967; Johnson 1964). Deposits in rockshelters, even though they are excellently preserved, do not exceed 4 m in depth and often present a very complex and somewhat mixed stratigraphy that results from both intensive human activity and from burrowing animals (Thomas 1983). Cultural materials in alluvial terraces at Arenosa Shelter and the Devils Mouth site were observed at depths exceeding 10 m below the ground surface (Dibble 1967). These sites are now inundated, but comparable alluvial terraces remain just below Amistad Dam. Sites 41VV661 and 41VV662 are located on that terrace and were discovered eroding out of a cutbank that was created by quarrying activity. These two sites have yielded sandy paste pottery and Perdiz points from their upper levels. Site 41VV661 exceeds 5 m in depth, and is a stratified, multicomponent site with seven vertically discrete cultural zones (Collins et al. 2000). Stratified sites located in alluvial terraces are so informative that they should be considered to have a very high potential to contribute to chronometric studies in the region. Any ground-disturbing activities that are planned for any alluvial terrace on the Rio Grande should be preceded by subsurface investigations and should be continuously monitored by an archaeologist. Alluvial terraces below Amistad Dam have the highest potential for containing open sites with important chronometric information of any area within or adjacent to the park.

CONCLUSION

The inventory of cultural resources within and adjacent to Amistad NRA constitutes a unique record of hunter-gatherer archeology. There are few if any places in North America or the world where so many sheltered sites and pictographs occur. For example, there are a total of 183 sheltered sites with preserved midden deposits in the ASMIS database. These midden deposits are as much as 3 m deep and contain desiccated plant and animal remains, basketry, traps, snares, sandals, wooden artifacts, and other cultural materials seldom preserved at archeological sites (Shafer 1986; Turpin 1995). Likewise, pictograph features are extremely abundant. Many of these pictographs are not solitary motifs, but rather are extremely complex, polychromatic panels that measure several meters in length and height (Boyd 1996, 1998b; Turpin 1995). A total of 109 pictograph panels have been identified in the current database within an area covering about 10,000 acres, and that is only a small sample of what is present in the region. There are few areas with such a rich and unusual inventory of cultural resources related to hunting and gathering groups.

It is ironic that the rich cultural resources of the region have been so neglected in recent years. There have been no large-scale excavations in the region by any institution since the work at Baker Cave (41VV213) in the early 1980s (Chadderdon 1983). No large-scale excavations have been conducted on federal lands in the region since Amistad Reservoir was impounded in 1967. Twenty-five years ago, Anderson (1974) noted that data deficiencies included the excavation of open sites beyond the margins of canyons, of which many are located within park boundaries.

Although several small-scale surveys and testing efforts have been completed, the SAIP pedestrian-level surveys conducted within and adjacent to Amistad NRA constitute the only large-scale archeological project of any type undertaken within the region during the last 15 years. Interestingly, the state of our knowledge of cultural resources within the park probably results from the limited time that Amistad NRA has been officially recognized as a part of the National Park System. Between 1965 and 1990, NPS had a presence at the reservoir but lacked a legislative mandate. As a result, NPS has had but a relatively brief history within the Amistad NRA   a history that spans a little over 10 years. Efforts to complete the archeological inventory of this extraordinary area has a short history and much work remains to be accomplished.

Appendix A

TASK DIRECTIVE FOR ARCHEOLOGICAL SURVEY DICTATED BY PL101-628 (Rewrite No. 5)

PROJECT AREA

Amistad National Recreation Area is located 12 miles northwest of Del Rio, Texas. Built across the Rio Grande, Amistad Dam impounds waters from the Pecos, Devils, and Rio Grande. The park's current boundary is the 1144.3 foot (above mean sea level) contour line adjacent to the reservoir. The boundary can be conceived of as an imaginary line, about 27 feet above normal reservoir level, that extends roughly 540 miles around the sinuous shoreline of the U.S. side of the reservoir.

The survey area for this project is "..the immediate vicinity of the recreation area" (PL101-628, Sec. 506, Sec. C). The "immediate vicinity" is interpreted to mean shorelines, river terraces, intervening side canyons, cliff faces, and upland areas adjacent to the park's current 1144.3' boundary.

PURPOSE OF THIS STUDY

Public Law 101-628 (Nov. 28, 1990) recognized the need for the Park Service to manage both the recreational and cultural resources adjacent to Amistad International Reservoir. The Legislation allows the Park Service to expand the current boundaries at Amistad National Recreation Area to a maximum of 58,500 acres (current size is about 57,400) for the purpose of protecting significant cultural resources. This legislation requires that:

> "The Secretary shall conduct a survey of the cultural resources in the immediate vicinity of
> the recreation area", and, that "Not later than two years after the date of enactment of this Act
> [Nov. 29, 1990], the Secretary shall submit a report to the Committee on Interior and Insular
> Affairs on the results of the survey."

The purpose of this study is to conduct the archeological survey and prepare the report of survey dictated by PL101-628.

SCOPE OF THE PROJECT

The primary purpose of the field survey is to identify the total range of cultural resources present within the area of survey, define their exact locations, determine their integrity and condition, and evaluate their significance. Determinations of eligibility for nomination to the National Register of Historical Places will *not* be made as part of this survey. The results of the field survey will be presented in an technical survey report which will be submitted to the Southwest Cultural Resources Center in the Spring of 1993.

LEVEL OF INVESTIGATIONS

This project is considered to be an *Identification Study* (NPS 28, Draft Release No. 4, December 91, page 29), a study designed to locate and document all possible cultural sites within the given area. The scope of the fieldwork will be limited to an intensive, reconnaissance level, pedestrian survey that will not involve subsurface testing or the collection of artifact samples.

PREVIOUS RESEARCH IN THE STUDY AREA

The study area for this project is part of a larger area known as the *Lower Pecos River Archeological Region*. This region in the most intensively and extensively researched cultural region in Texas. The first "scientific" excavations occurred in the late 1920s. By the late 1930s, five major research institutions were working in the region. During the 1940s, the pace of research slackened but increased again following WW II.

In the late 1950s, the United States and Mexico jointly began the construction of Amistad Dam. Prior to inundation of the area (1969), the National Park Service funded a major study (1958-1970) which inventoried many of the well-known archeological and historical resources that would be affected by the creation of Amistad Reservoir. The current project area is roughly the same as that of the pre-inundation study. Twenty-two major archeological sites were excavated and over 300 major rockshelter, river terrace, and rock art sites were inventoried as part of the pre-inundation study. To date, approximately 500-600 archeological sites have been documented in the immediate vicinity of Amistad Reservoir.

OVERVIEW OF REGIONAL HISTORY

The prehistory of the Lower Pecos River Region has been well documented by the numerous archeological and scientific excavations. As early as the 1930s, the Smithsonian Institution was excavating rockshelters along the Pecos River to obtain museum and research specimens. The accumulated data from the last 50 years indicates that the first humans arrived in the park area at the end of the last Ice Age about 11,000 years ago. At Bonfire Shelter, adjacent to the Rio Grande, archeologists have excavated the remains of hundreds of Ice Age bison (now extinct) that were stampeded about 10,500 years ago over a cliff by an organized group of Paleoindian hunters. The site represents the oldest known example of the bison jump technique of hunting in the New World.

In addition to the amazing archeological materials in the dry rockshelters, the Lower Pecos River region contains some of the largest and oldest prehistoric pictographic rock art in the nation. With over 250 pictograph sites in the region, the area is also among the densest concentrations of Archaic rock art in North America. Some pictograph sites consist of only one or two small painted images in red or black. Other sites contain multiple panels, with 4 meter tall images, in polychromatic colors, that stretch over 30 meters along the rear wall of a shelter. Researchers have defined several distinct styles for the rock art some of which have been radiocarbon dated to 3865-4450 years ago.

The last vestiges of the Ice Age environment and associated plants and animals in the region appear to have been gone by at least 8,500 years ago. With this change in environmental resources, the economic strategies and subsistence patterns for the ever increasing regional population likewise had to change. The archeological evidence indicates that a shift from a highly mobile, big game hunting, lifeway to a semi-sedentary broad spectrum gathering of plant resources and small game hunting occurred as a result of environmental change. There does not appear to have been a consistent reliance on any one specific animal or

plant. This broad spectrum subsistence regime appears to have continued, with only minor changes or technological innovations, almost up until the coming of the first Europeans. Throughout most of prehistory, there is little archeological evidence to infer that any regular trade networks existed with other culture areas in the United States or Northern Mexico. By the end of the 19th century, the Apache and later the Comanche traversed the region.

Costaño de Sosa is generally acknowledged as being the first European to explore the Lower Pecos Region. In 1590, accompanied by his troops, de Sosa traveled from Montclova, Mexico up the Rio Grande Valley to the Pecos River, then on to the Pecos Pueblo in northern New Mexico. Costaño de Sosa's account of this expedition represents the first written narrative of the Lower Pecos River region. Researchers generally use the date of 1590 as the end of prehistory and the beginning of history in the Middle Rio Grande Valley.

History, in the European sense of time, may have begun during 16th century but there are few documents and even fewer physical evidences of European presence up until about the mid-19th century. From the 16th century to 1821, the present-day park area belonged to Spain. Mexico was granted independence from Spain in 1821, and, with the Treaty of Guadalupe Hidalgo in 1846, it ceded the land to the Republic of Texas which, in 1847, became the 28th state to join the United States. Although part of Texas, there were no real economic or ethnic changes in the region until after the Civil War ended.

By 1875, the U.S. Army, using an ancient Indian trail, had completed the first wagon trail across the Pecos River at its mouth with the Rio Grande. The east-bank portion of this trail is located within the park. In the early 1880s, construction of a transcontinental railroad across the southern United States was in full swing. The route would eventually connect San Diego and New Orleans. In 1881-1882, more than 8,000 laborers (Germans, Italians, Mexicans, African-Americans, and Chinese) were building grades and laying track between the towns of Shumla and Del Rio in southwest Texas. On January 12, 1883, east and west sections of the first southern transcontinental railroad were joined with a silver spike about one mile north of the mouth of the Pecos at the Rio Grande.

The Southern Pacific Railroad built a station between Tunnel No. 1 (the first railroad tunnel in Texas) and the fair-weather bridge across of the mouth of the Pecos. The station was named Painted Caves for the prehistoric Indian paintings in three nearby rockshelters. Today, Painted Caves Station is known as Parida Cave which is operated by the Park Service (under agreement with the private landowners) as an interpretive site for park visitors.

With the coming of the Southern Pacific to southwest Texas in 1883, Val Verde County was carved out of two adjoining counties and the small town of Del Rio was made the county seat in 1885. The railroad used the town as its regional headquarters. The first major wave of European settlers came to southwest Texas as small towns such as Pumpville, Double Tanks, Loma Alta, Comstock, Langtry, and Shumla sprang up adjacent to the railroad tracks. Judge Roy Bean, "Law West of the Pecos" set up his bar room (the Jersey Lily) and courthouse in Langtry. The sheep and goat ranching industry expanded rapidly as the railroad brought economic prosperity to the entire region which continued up through the Great Depression almost until World War II.

ETHNOGRAPHIC SYNOPSIS

Amistad NRA has never had an ethnographic overview and assessment performed. However, the existing literature (Campbell 1988; Hester 1989a, 1989b; Newcomb 1961; Salinas 1990; Turpin 1984, 1989; Weddle 1976) on the current project area indicates that there is very little ethnographic or historic information concerning any Native American Groups at, or after, European contact in 1590.

The first known Native American Groups in the region appeared after the Pueblo Revolt of 1680. They were transient Plains Indian groups who traversed the Trans-Pecos area (between Big Bend NP and Amistad NRA) to raid Spanish settlements in northern Mexico. The Apache, Comanche, and Kiowa are known to have traveled through the Trans-Pecos region during the 17-19th centuries. There are no known Native American Groups that currently claim any portion of southwest Texas or northern Mexico as sacred lands, as an ancestral homeland, or as the loci for traditional activities.

DISTRIBUTION OF ARCHEOLOGICAL SITES IN THE PROJECT AREA

There are about 500-600 known archeological sites in the immediate vicinity of Amistad Reservoir. Of this number, roughly 150 are intermittently or permanently inundated under the waters of the reservoir. There is one site and four National Register Archeological Districts that are within or immediately adjacent to the National Recreation Area. The one site is the Rattlesnake Canyon Pictograph in Rattlesnake Canyon near Langtry. The National Register Districts are: (1) West of Pecos Railroad Camp District [12 sites]; (2) Mile Canyon District [3 sites]; Lower Pecos Canyon District [72 sites]; Seminole Canyon Archeological District [84 sites].

Using existing literature, a generalized predictive model was developed for this project. There are at least six different types of sites which will be documented by the survey crews; dry and wet rockshelters, pictograph sites, river terrace sites, U. S. Military sites, Southern Pacific Railroad sites, and Early Ranching sites. It is highly unlikely that any Historic Native American or Spanish Colonial sites will be identified. About 95% of all sites will be prehistoric in age, dating anywhere from 9500 B.C. to A.D. 1400-1500. Upwards of 75% of all sites investigated during the project will be rockshelters situated in cliff canyon walls. Approximately 45-50 pictograph sites and a couple of petroglyph sites are known to exist in the survey area.

WORK TO BE PERFORMED DURING THIS PROJECT

1. *Archival Research*: The Texas Archeological Research Laboratory (TARL) at the University of Texas at Austin, is the primary archival repository for archeological data in the State of Texas. TARL assigns permanent site trinomial numbers and maintains site records and map plottings for every site in the State. The major shortcoming of TARL data is that a researcher can not tell from the available records where previous investigators have already searched for sites. This deficiency makes it impossible to avoid some duplication of fieldwork.

    This project has been careful to record exactly where they have surveyed, supplying negative information as well as positive information. While this requires more time than previous investigators have been willing to allow, the approach is considerably more scientific and reflects the standards established for National Park Service projects. The major shortcoming of the park's existing data base is that much of the data is more than 20 years old. The park has photographs, site forms, accurate locational data, and site maps for less than 150 sites.

Another major shortcoming of the current archeological data base is that the park has absolutely no data at all for some portions of the survey area. Three specific geographic areas need to be researched: [1] the upper Rio Grande above the town of Langtry, about 8 miles of river shoreline, cliffs, and side canyons; [2] the upper Pecos River, about 5-6 miles, on both sides of the river, of cliffs and intervening side canyons; [3] the Rio Grande between buoys 4-28, about 15 miles of river valley with relatively few side canyons. After discussions with archeologists that have conducted research in these three areas, there is no doubt that many sites exist but are unrecorded.

A literature search for reports, articles, and books pertaining to the project area will also be necessary. There are over 150 reports which deal directly with the cultural resources within the project area. In addition, there are more than one hundred "grey literature" reports which pertain to the archeology in the project area. There is no one complete listing of NPS studies or surveys which have occurred within the existing park boundaries. A complete annotated bibliography of all reports will be a by-product of this project.

2.   *Field work:* The field work for this project presents a whole series of unique logistical situations not commonly found in archeological fieldwork. In almost cases, survey crews will use a boat to get to designated areas. More than 90% of the survey area consists of sheer cliff walls and densely vegetated canyon bottoms. Daily temperatures commonly exceed 100☐ for weeks at a time. The remoteness of most areas on the upper Rio Grande and Pecos River will require survey crews to camp for extended periods. Otherwise, crews will spend nearly half of the work day traveling to/from certain survey areas. Survey Crews will work 10 on/4 off schedules to meet the need for extended surveys in remote areas.

National Archeological Survey Initiative (NASI) level documentation is used for previously recorded sites targeted for acquisition. The fieldwork consists of preparing a scale site map, completion of site data forms, completion of a project management evaluation, videotape photography of pictographs and other significant archeological features, and determinations of site elevation and UTM coordinates. Back in the office, the field data is added to the existing map sets and computer files. Rock art videotape is printed out and added to the hard copy site files.

Reconnaissance level documentation is used for newly identified sites in areas where no sites are currently known to exist and at sites listed as "possible targets" for acquisition. The fieldwork consists of identification, issuance of a temporary site numbers, plotting site locations on project base maps, noting the presence or absence of significant archeological features, and videotaping of rock art for archives. Reconnaissance level documentation produces only the most basic information about a site whereas NASI level documentation produces data sufficient for determinations of eligibility to the National Register and meets the standards of the Park Service's Cultural Sites Inventory.

For the purpose of this survey, the areas to be surveyed have been divided into about 400 different *Archeological Management Units* (AMUs). An AMU consists of a discrete geographical unit divided from adjacent AMUs by intervening side canyons so no two AMUs are of equal size. Some AMUs are known to contain numerous previously documented sites while other AMUs have no sites listed at all. Some AMUs have a high degree of potential for sites while others have very little potential. Some AMUs are accessible by boat; others can only be reached overland by a 4-wheel drive vehicle.

Each AMU has been researched to determine if any previously recorded sites exist within the area. We have been able to eliminate roughly 50% of the known sites from consideration for acquisition using archival research alone. Some sites are classified as "possible targets" due to incomplete documentation. Others cannot be evaluated because little or no documentation exists and will require an onsite evaluation.

Each AMU has also been evaluated as to its archeological potential for unrecorded sites. This rating is based on the geology, soil type(s), topographic setting, percentage and type of vegetative cover, previous archeological work in the immediate vicinity, and personal experiences of the field crew. No two AMUs have the same archeological potential or will require an equal amount of time to survey.

Prehistoric pictographs and petroglyphs are know to exist at more than 45 sites. Some rock art panels contain one or two small figures while other panels may extend more than 50 meters along a rockshelter wall and reach heights of 6 meters above the ground surface. Rock art documentation is very labor intensive and can produce volumes of archival data. Traditional documentation methods range from taking a single picture to preparing detailed measured drawings of the entire site. Of the 45 known sites, only 6 have measured drawings. Most sites have had "selected" panels photographed, only 6 sites have been completely photographed. Park Service standards require that this project document 100% of the rock art at each site.

This project has developed a special method for documenting rock art using computers that addresses most of the problems associated with traditional rock art field methods --inaccurate renderings, archival management, expense and intensive labor. At each site, this project videotapes the entire rockshelter wall. Back in the office, computer software is utilized to manipulate video images (at the pixel level if necessary) allowing researchers to identify even the faintest of images. Anything seen on the monitor can be printed out or saved on floppy disk, thus reducing the amount and types of archives produced for each site. Exact drawings of any pictograph at any site can be accomplished in a matter of minutes. Spatial, thematic, temporal, and distributional studies of the rock art will now be possible for the first time.

The bulk of the field personnel for this project will come from Amistad's Archeological Volunteer-in-the-Park (VIP) Program. The total project area will be divided into a number discrete geographic survey areas. Each area will be surveyed by a crew consisting of an NPS Archeologist Crew Chief and up to 10 VIPs. If no VIPs are available, the project will put two crews in the field composed of NPS personnel.

3. *National Register Evaluation:* National Register of Historic Property (NRHP) determinations will not be made as part of this project. However, sufficient data will be collected so that at some future date eligibility determinations could be made. A separate 10-238 package for National Register submissions will be prepared during FY93.

4. *Archival Data Management:* This project will generate a tremendous amount of data which will be compiled in several different mediums (film archives, computer files, and hard copy paperwork). The photographic archives (35mm and videotape) will be inventoried, accessioned, and cataloged using a non-NPS, IBM compatible, computer software program; the park currently does not use Automated National Catalog System (ANCS) to catalog photographs or video. At some future date, a dBASE conversion program can be written to convert the film archives into the ANCS cataloging system. The

data contained on field forms and daily logs will be entered into a computer using dBASE. All computer files are backed-up on a weekly basis using floppy disks. A master set of discs will be stored off-site. Hard copy archives (maps, drawings, completed forms, photograph prints) will be stored in acid-free file folders in a fire-resistant file cabinet. With the completion of the project, all project files will be microfiched, with copies going to the Southwest Cultural Resources Center, Texas Archeological Research Center, and the Texas Historical Commission.

5. *Curation:* The fieldwork phase of the project will be conducted on non-Park Service lands. Therefore, there will be no field specimens or artifactual materials collected which need to be cataloged using the Automated National Catalog System (ANCS). Archival documentation generated by this project will be accessioned into the park's museum collection following completion of the project.

6. *Cultural Sites Inventory (CSI)Update*: The field forms for this project have been designed to incorporate the various data fields that are contained in Cultural Sites Inventory (CSI). Since only prototype software for the CSI is currently available, it will not be possible to update the CSI even though the data will have been collected. At some future date, the CSI could be updated but it will not be part of this project.

EXPECTED PRODUCTS FROM THIS PROJECT

1. *Project Summary:* The Project Coordinator, Southwest Regional Office, will be kept informed as to the progress of the project by way of regular phone calls from the Principle Investigator. A preliminary report on sites targeted for acquisition will be prepared for the Lands Acquisition Office (Harlan Hobbs) by January 15, 1993. This report will contain tri-nominal site number, site size, landowner, priority for acquisition, and will be correlated to numbers on the proposed boundary expansion map.

2. *Draft Final Report:* A rough draft of the final report should be ready by about April 1, 1993. A copy of the structure of this report is attached.

3. *Final Report:* June 1, 1993

   a. Archeological site data forms: All original site data forms will be maintained at park level. A microfiche copy of the project papers will be forwarded to the Southwest Cultural Resources Center, Santa Fe, the Texas Historical Commission, Austin Texas, and the Texas Archeological Research Laboratory, the University of Texas at Austin.

   b. Site location maps: All original maps associated with this project will be maintained at park level. Locational data for sites identified by this survey is protected by the Freedom of Information Act from public disclosure.

   c. Disposition of field records and photographs: All original project materials will be curated at park level and will be maintained in an environmentally controlled storage area.

   d. Disposition of field equipment: All field equipment, computers, and office equipment acquired by this project will remain at the park permanently assigned to the Park Archeologist.

PERSONNEL INVOLVED IN THE PROJECT

Regional Office Project Supervisor: Jim Mayberry, Supervisory Archeologist, Southwest Region

Amistad Project Administrator: Eldon Kohlman, Management Assistant

Principal Investigator: Joseph H. Labadie, Park Archeologist, Amistad National Recreation Area

Field Personnel: Frank Garcia, Archeology Technician; Tom Dureka, Archeology Technician; Ann Mesrobian, Archeology Technician.

Research Consultants (non-salaried): The project will have a number of non-salaried consultants, they are:

Archeology: Dr. Thomas R. Hester, Director, Texas Archeological Research Laboratory (TARL), the University of Texas at Austin; Dr. Solveig A. Turpin, Associate Director, TARL-UTA; Dr. Grant Hall, Anthropology Dept. Texas Tech University; Dr. E. Mott Davis, University of Texas at Austin.

Rock Art Preservation: Dr. Marvin Rowe, Chairman Dept. of Chemistry, Texas A&M University; Dr. John Russ, Dept. of Chemistry, Sam Houston State University; Dr. Frank Bock, Chairman, American Rock Art Research Association (ARARA), San Miguel, CA; Dr. Ken Hedges, Chief Curator, San Diego Museum of Man.

Photography: Gay Parrish, KERA-TV (PBS), Dallas Texas. Bud Hampton, still photographer, Estes Park Colorado; Jim Zintgraff, still photographer, San Antonio.

Flora/Faunal Macrofossils: Dr. Carl Rheinhard, Dept. of Anthropology, University of Nebraska at Lincoln; Dr. Alan Wright, Dept. of Anthropology, University of Nebraska at Lincoln; Mr. Jeff Huebner, Doctoral Candidate, University of Texas at Austin.

Report and Publication: Dr. John Labadie, Dept. of Art (layout and design), University of Cincinnati; Kelly Scott, Editor (desktop publishing), Texas Archeological Research Laboratory (TARL), University of Texas at Austin.

Attachment No.1. Proposed structure for Archeological Survey Report

INTRODUCTION
(General overview of project and report organization)

MANAGEMENT SUMMARY
(Who, what, when, where, and why for the project)

DESCRIPTION OF STUDY AREA
(Exact area covered by project)

ENVIRONMENT
        (Paleoenvironmental reconstructions, modern flora/fauna)

RESEARCH GOALS AND STRATEGIES
        Previous Research (highlights/problems)
        Research design for project
        Methods of data collection
        Pictograph documentation
        Archival Management

OVERVIEW OF REGIONAL HISTORY
        (this section of report contracted to Dr. Solveig Turpin) will focus on regional chronologies for archeology and rock art; detailed discussion on cultural periods and artifact assemblages; subsistence strategies (and ethnographic analogies) and how they changed over time). This section will be broken down into the major cultural periods for the project area: Paleoindian, Archaic (early, middle, late, transitional), Late Prehistoric, Historic Native Americans (Ethnographic Synopsis), Spanish Colonial, U.S. Military, Southern Pacific Era, Early Ranching.

SUMMARY OF FIELD INVESTIGATIONS
        Summary of natural/cultural impacts to sites
        Discussion of rock art deterioration
        Inventory of sites investigated

RECOMMENDATIONS FOR LAND ACQUISITIONS
        (Tabular listing of sites recommended for land acquistion)

REFERENCES CITED

Appendix B

SURVEY MODEL

Purpose
> To identify sites in draw-down zone.

Location
> Given the size of the potential survey area (540 miles of shoreline) it will not be possible to conduct a 100% area survey.

> 1. Discussions with Rangers as to where "high traffic" areas are within a particular district.

> 2. Areas with high "archaeological potential" regardless of visitation levels.

Archaeological Potential

> There is a direct correlation between the occurrence of archaeological sites and topographic zones adjacent to Amistad Reservoir. Pre-inundation research in the three major river valleys that form Amistad Reservoir demonstrated that certain topographic features have greater archeological potential than others. For example, large fire-cracked rock features are more likely to occur on the colluvial terraces adjacent to the confluence of main river channels and intervening side canyons than they are along any other portion of the side canyons. Or, that (in general) the greater the distance away from canyon rims, the lower the probability for surface lithic scatters. Or, that pictograph and petroglyph sites are most often found in steep-walled canyon areas adjacent to main river drainages or at the confluences of intervening side canyons. It has also been demonstrated that certain pictograph styles (ex. Red Monochrome) usually occur in the same topographic setting. So, the archaeological potential for a given area is linked to the pre-inundation topographic setting.

> *1.Terrace* -- zones of overlapping occupation, with a wide variety of artifacts made from non-perishable materials.

> *2.Canyon Walls* -- rockshelters with preserved macrobotanical deposits and/or pictographs.

> *3.Uplands* -- discrete areas of occupation which often are limited in artifact variety.

> *4.Springs*   sites are confined to immediate areas or adjacent to springs.

> *5.Confluences* -- sites include fire-cracked rock features and lithic scatters.

Priorities

> Exposed terraces to main river channels
> Junction of intervening side canyons with rivers
> Areas with exposed cliff faces
> Upland areas adjacent to canyons

- Existing back country camping areas
  Recent roadways across any areas that are normally inundated
- Proposed back country camping areas listed in draft Back Country Management Plan
- Areas adjacent to springs

Field Procedures

Archeological field work conducted by AmeriCorps personnel will follow a logical progression of tasks. Six basic steps have been identified and are detailed below.

STEP ONE

Step One represents office work. Office work will be scheduled for Mondays, Wednesdays, and Fridays. It involves the initial selection of a geographically defined area for survey and a series of tasks that must be completed prior to the actual field work:

    determine physical limits of survey
    photocopy International Boundary and Water Commission map areas for survey
    determine equipment/logistics needed for survey
    contact appropriate Amistad divisions for assistance one week in advance
    e.mail Amistad divisions 2 days in advance of field work

STEP TWO

Step two represents the initial field reconnaissance of the area defined in step one. Field work will be scheduled for Tuesdays and Thursdays:

    can be accomplished by one field crew member; two is preferred
    when sites are discovered, first task is to define the total areal extent of the cultural materials on field maps, assign temporary site number, create sketch map in field notebook
    for small sites, all documentation will be completed at time of discovery before continuing the survey. This includes sites forms, mapping, photography, and artifact collection.
    for large sites, initial reconnaissance documentation will be completed and a second follow-up trip will be scheduled (with all crew members participating) to complete the job.

STEP THREE

Step three represents office work generated by the previous day's field work:

    for large sites, schedule return trip for field work within two weeks of discovery
    for small sites, finalize all documentation; update appropriate databases, files, map sets.
    arrange for photocopies of completed site form and map plottings; send to Chief Ranger within one week of field work

STEP FOUR

Step four represents the follow-up field work at large or complex sites:
notify appropriate Amistad divisions by e.mail 2 days in advance of field work
complete scheduled fieldwork at large or complex sites (site forms, photography, mapping, and artifact collection.

STEP FIVE

Step Five represents the office work generated from the previous day's field work at large sites not documented during initial reconnaissance (Step Two):

-finalize paperwork from field work at large sites (site forms, mapping, photography, and artifact collection)

STEP SIX

In Step 6 arrange for photocopies and make distributions of completed site form and map plottings; begin all over again at Step One.

PAPERWORK ASSOCIATED WITH FIELDWORK

There are three primary planning aspects to archeological field work: (1) the administrative and logistical planning that occurs before entering the field; (2) the actual time spent in the field looking for archeological sites, and; 3) the post field work administrative tasks. For each archeological site discovered during fieldwork, the following tasks have been identified:

1. Maintain field journals and logs for film and site numbers, and notes on daily basis each time fieldwork occurs;

2. Map work
a. Plot areas surveyed on International Boundary and Water Commission maps and define exact site areas
b. USGS 7.5' topographic maps: plot sites on park's Archaeological Base Maps
c. Calculate UTMs for sites from 7.5' topographic maps
d. Original field maps/survey area maps archived in a single map set

3. Site Form Package
a. Complete basic 3-page site form
b. Complete scaled site plan map detailing horizontal relationships among archaeological features
c. Attach photocopy of 7.5' topographic map location
d. Complete mortar hole form when appropriate
e. Complete photo log; use mug board in photos
f. Update computer data base using TexSite software

4. Distribution of paperwork
a. Copies to Ranger Division
b. Site form package to Texas Archeological Research Laboratory for permanent VV # (end of project)
c. Create site folder for Cultural Sites Inventory files

5. Artifact Collection
a. All diagnostics will be collected at each site
b. Field specimen number will be assigned with log maintained
c. Collected materials bagged by site number and maintained in temporary accession storage area

6. Photography
a. All photos will use mug boards/scale
b. Photo log and film-roll log
c. Small sites done during initial survey; large sites during second site visit
d. Processed film filed in site folders

Appendix C

AMISTAD NATIONAL RECREATION AREA
SAIP ARCHAEOLOGICAL SURVEY 1991/1992
SITE FORM

41VV_____ **NPS/AMIS:**_____ **Other Designation:**_____

IBWC Map:_____ **USGS 7.5' QUAD:**_____

UTM Z (N) 14_____ **(E)**_____ **Elev.**_____(ft.)_____(m)

Drainage: Pecos   Rio Grande   Devils River   Tributary_____

Description of Site Location:

_____
_____
_____

Site Description:_____
_____
_____
_____

Site Type: Open   Cliff Shelter   Rockshelter   Cave

Other_____

Site Dimensions (m):_____X_____ **Orientation (mag. north):**_____deg.

Estimated Depth of Deposit (cm):_____ **Artifact Density (circle one):** High   Medium   Low

FEATURES OBSERVED

Burned Rock   Ash/Charcoal   Grinding Facet Boulder Metate Pictograph* (circle one)

Midden   Stone Circle   Incised Groove Cupule Other_____

Hearth   Lithic Scatter   Mortar Hole   Petroglyph   _____

Discussion of Features:_____
_____
_____
_____

ROCK ART

*Pecos River Style   Bold Line Geometric   Red Linear   Red Monochrome   Historic

Indeterminate

C.1

Comment:

_____

_____

Photos: Color: NO YES Roll:_____   B/W: NO YES Roll:_____

Slides: NO YES Roll:_____   Video: NO YES Roll:_____

ARTIFACTS

(circle items observed)

Lithics		**Bone**	**Vegetal**	**Field Sack:**
Debitage	Bifacial	Burned	Mat Sandal	Accession # AMIS_____
Core	Blank	Incised	Basket Tool Bag	# Provenience
Hammerstone	Preform	Tool	Cordage	_____ _____
Unifacial	Knife	Other:	Other:_____	_____ _____
Modified Flake	Dart Point			_____ _____
Side Scraper	Arrow Point	**Groundstone**	**Exotic Material**	_____ _____
End Scraper	Other:_____	Mano Metate	_____	_____ _____
Graver	_____	Pestle	_____	_____ _____
Burin	_____	Mussel shell	_____	_____ _____

Discussion of Artifacts:_____

_____

_____

_____

_____

VEGETATION

Plant	Density	Plant	Density	Plant	Density
_____	L-M-H	_____	L-M-H	_____	L-M-H
_____	L-M-H	_____	L-M-H	_____	L-M-H

Has site been previously inundated? YES   NO

Comment: _____

IMPACTS

Vandalism Rodent Disturbance Erosion Livestock Vegetation   Other (visitor usage, modern hearth)

Discussion:_____

_____

_____

_____

Additional Comments:

_____
_____
_____
_____
_____
_____
_____
_____
_____
_____
_____
_____
_____

Recorded by:_____ **Date:**_____**Total Hrs:**_____

Appendix D

AMISTAD NATIONAL RECREATION AREA
LOW-WATER ARCHAEOLOGICAL SURVEY--1994/1995
SITE FORM

41VV_____ NPS/AMIS:_____ Other Designation:_____

IBWC Map:_____ USGS 7.5' QUAD:_____

UTM Z (N) 14_____ (E)_____ Elev._____(ft.)_____(m)

Drainage: Pecos _____Rio Grande _____Devils _____Tributary_____

Description of Site Location:

_____

_____

_____

Site Description:_____

_____

_____

_____

Site Type: Open   Cliff Shelter   Rockshelter   Cave
Other_____

Site Dimensions (m):_____X_____ **Orientation (mag. north):**_____deg.

Estimated Depth of Deposit (cm):_____ **Artifact Density (circle one):** High Medium Low

FEATURES OBSERVED

Burned Rock   Ash/Charcoal   Grinding Facet Boulder Metate Pictograph* (circle one)

Midden   Stone Circle   Incised Groove Cupule Other_____

Hearth   Lithic Scatter Mortar Hole   Petroglyph   _____

Discussion of Features:_____

_____

_____

Comment:_____

Photos: Color: NO   YES   Roll:_____   B/W: NO   YES   Roll:_____

Slides: NO   YES   Roll:_____   Video: NO   YES   Roll:_____

Digital: NO   YES

ARTIFACTS

(circle items observed)

Lithics

Debitage	Bifacial
Core	Blank
Hammerstone	Preform
Unifacial	Knife
Modified Flake	Dart Point
Side Scraper	Arrow Point
End Scraper	Other:_____
Graver	_____
Burin	_____

Bone

Burned
Incised
Tool
Other:
_____

Groundstone

Mano   Metate
Pestle
Mussel shell

Vegetal   **Field Sack:**

Mat Sandal   Accession # AMIS_____
Basket Tool Bag # Provenience
Cordage   _____ _____
Other:_____ _____ _____
_____ _____ _____

Exotic Material_____ _____
_____ _____ _____
_____ _____ _____
_____ _____ _____

Discussion of Artifacts:_____
_____
_____
_____

VEGETATION

Plant	Density	Plant	Density	Plant	Density
_____	L-M-H	_____	L-M-H	_____	L-M-H
_____	L-M-H	_____	L-M-H	_____	L-M-H

Has site been previously inundated? YES   NO
Comment:_____
_____

IMPACTS

Vandalism   Rodent Disturbance   Erosion   Livestock Vegetation Other (camping, visitor usage)
Discussion:_____
_____
_____
_____

SUMMARY COMMENTS:
_____
_____
_____
_____
_____

Recorded by:_____ **Date:**_____ **Total Hrs:**_____

ARPA Patrol Data

Monitoring Priority (circle one);

High: high visitation area; high artifact visibility; high archaeological/scientific integrity/importance;

Med. High: frequently visited area; artifacts are visible, near other medium or above priority ranked archaeological sites; high archaeological/scientific integrity/importance;

Medium: far from visitor access; hidden by vegetation; artifact visibility is low, more than 50% archaeological/scientific integrity remains;

Med. Low: far from visitor accessibility; artifact visibility is very low; most archaeological/scientific integrity is destroyed;

Low: Site is destroyed (by nature, inundation, other), and no integrity remains

Explain selection of priority category:

_____
_____
_____
_____
_____

REFERENCES CITED

Alexander, Robert K.

    1970   *Archeological Investigations at Parida Cave, Val Verde County, Texas.* Papers of the Texas Archeological Salvage Project 19. University of Texas, Austin.

    1974   *The Archeology of Conejo Shelter: A Study of Cultural Stability at an Archaic Rockshelter Site in Southwestern Texas.* Ph.D. dissertation, Department of Anthropology, The University of Texas at Austin.

Amos, Bonnie B., and Frederick R. Gehlbach (ed.)

    1988   *Edwards Plateau Vegetation: Plant Ecological Studies in Texas.* Baylor University Press, Waco, Texas.

Anderson, Bruce A.

    1974   *An Archeological Assessment of the Amistad Recreation Area.* Branch of Cultural Research, National Park Service, Sante Fe.

Andrews, R.L., and J.M. Adovasio

    1980   *Perishable Industries from Hinds Cave, Val Verde County, Texas.* Ethnology Monographs Number 5. Department of Anthropology, University of Pittsburgh.

Arbingast, S.A., L. Kennamer, R. Ryan, J. Buchanan, W. Hezlep, L. Ellis, T. Jordan, C. Granger, and C. Zlatkovich

    1976   *Atlas of Texas.* Bureau of Business Research, The University of Texas at Austin.

Archer, Steve

    1990   Development and Stability of Grass/Woody Mosaics in a Subtropical Savanna Parkland, Texas, U.S.A. *Journal of Biogeography* 17:453-462.

    1995   Tree-grass Dynamics in a *Prosopis*-Thornscrub Savannah Parkland: Reconstructing the Past and Predicting the Future. *Ecoscience* 2(1):84-99.

Archer, Steve, Charles Scifres, C.R. Bassham, and Robert Maggio

    1988   Autogenic Succession in a Subtropical Savannah: Conversion of Grassland to Thorn Woodland. *Ecological Monographs* 58(2):111-127.

Barnes, Virgil

    1977   *Del Rio Sheet, Geologic Atlas of Texas, Robert Thomas Hill Memorial Edition.* Bureau of Economic Geology, The University of Texas at Austin.

Bement, Leland C.

    1989   Lower Pecos Canyonlands. In *From the Gulf to the Rio Grande: Human Adaptation in Central, South, and Lower Pecos Texas,* by T.R. Hester, S.L. Black, D.G. Steele, B.W. Olive, A.A. Fox, K.J. Reinhard, and L.C. Bement, pp. 63-76. Research Series No. 33. Arkansas Archeological Survey, Fayetteville.

Bement, Leland C., and Solveig A. Turpin.
  1987   Technological Continuity and Functional Change: The Case of the Dorso End Scraper. *Plains Anthropologist* 32(116):191-196.

Binford, Lewis R.
  1980   Willow Smoke and Dogs' Tails: Hunter-Gatherer Settlement Systems and Archaeological Site Formation. *American Antiquity* 45:4-20.

  1982   The Archaeology of Place. *Journal of Anthropological Archaeology* 1:5-31.

Black, Stephen L.
  1986   *The Clemente and Hermina Hinojosa Site, 41JW8: A Toyah Horizon Campsite in Southern Texas.* Special Report No. 18. Center for Archaeological Research, The University of Texas at San Antonio.

  1989   South Texas Plains. In *From the Gulf to the Rio Grande: Human Adaptation in Central, South, and Lower Pecos Texas*, by Thomas R. Hester, Stephen L. Black D. Gentry Steele, Ben W. Olive, Anne A. Fox, Karl J. Reinhard, and Leland C. Bement, pp. 39-62. Arkansas Archeological Survey Research Series No. 33. Fayetteville, Arkansas.

  1997   Oven Cookery at the Honey Creek Site. In *Hot Rock Cooking on the Greater Edwards Plateau: Four Burned Rock Midden Sites in West Central Texas*, by S.L. Black, L.W. Ellis, D.G. Creel, and G.T. Goode, pp. 255-268. Studies in Archeology 22. Texas Archeological Research Laboratory, University of Texas, Austin.

Blair, W. Frank
  1950   The Biotic Provinces of Texas. *The Texas Journal of Science* 2:93-117.

Boyd, Carolyn E.
  1992   Archaic Codices of Along the Lower Pecos. Paper Presented at the 63rd Annual Meeting of the Texas Archeological Society, Corpus Christi, Texas.

  1996   Shamanic Journeys into the Otherworld of the Archaic Chichimec. *Latin American Antiquity* 7(2):152-164.

  1998a   Pictographic Evidence of Peyotism in the Lower Pecos Texas Archaic. In *The Archaeology of Rock-Art*, edited by C. Chippindale and P. Taçon. Pp. 229-246. Cambridge University Press. Cambridge.

  1998b   *The Work of Art: Rock Art and Adaptation in the Lower Pecos Texas Archaic.* Ph.D. dissertation, Department of Anthropology, Texas A&M University, College Station.

Boyd, Carolyn E., and J. Philip Dering
  1996   Medicinal and Hallucinogenic Plants Identified in the Sediments and Pictographs of the Lower Pecos, Texas Archaic. *Antiquity* 70(268):256-275.

Brown, David E.
  1982   Chihuahuan Desertscrub. *Desert Plants* 4:169-179.

Brown, Kenneth M.
    1991   Prehistoric Economics at Baker Cave: A Plan for Research. In *Papers on Lower Pecos Prehistory*, edited by Solveig A. Turpin, pp. 87-140.. Studies in Archeology No. 8. Texas Archeological Research Laboratory, The University of Texas at Austin.

Brune, Gunnar
    1981   *Springs of Texas.* Branch-Smith, Inc. Ft. Worth, Texas.

Bryant, Vaughn M., Jr.
    1969   *Late Full-Glacial and Post-Glacial Pollen Analysis of Texas Sediments.* Ph.D. dissertation, Department of Biology, The University of Texas at Austin.

    1974   Prehistoric Diet in Southwest Texas: The Coprolite Evidence. *American Antiquity* 39:407-420.

Bryant, Vaughn M., Jr., and Richard G. Holloway
    1985   A Late Quaternary Paleoenvironmental Record of Texas: An Overview of the Pollen Evidence. In *Pollen Records of Late Quaternary North American Sediments*, edited by V.M. Bryant and F.G. Holloway, pp. 39-70. American Association of Stratigraphic Palynologists Foundation, Dallas, Texas.

Chadderdon, Mary F.
    1983   *Baker Cave, Val Verde County, Texas: The 1976 Excavations.* Special Report No. 13. Center for Archaeological Research, The University of Texas at San Antonio.

Clary, Karen H.
    1997   Phylogeny, Character Evolution, and Biogeography of *Yucca* L. (Agavaceae) as Inferred from Plant Morphology and Sequences of the Internal Transcribed Spacer (ITS) Region of the Nuclear Ribosomal DNA. Ph.D. dissertation, Department of Botany, the University of Texas at Austin. Austin, Texas.

Collins, Michael B.
    1969   *Test Excavations at Amistad International Reservoir, Fall 1967.* Papers of the Texas Archeological Salvage Project No. 16. University of Texas, Austin.

Collins, Michael B., Joe Labadie, and Elton R. Prewitt
    2000   A Brief Account of the 1999 TAS Field School, Amistad National Recreation Area. *Texas Archaeology* 44:1. 9-17.

Davis, C.W., L.A. Karch, and D.H. Scovill
    1995   *Archeological Sites Management Information System (ASMIS) Definition.* U.S. Department of the Interior, National Park Service, Anthropology Division. Washington, D.C.

Dering, J. Phil
    1979   *Pollen and Plant Macrofossil Vegetation Record Recovered from Hinds Cave, Val Verde County, Texas.* Master's thesis, Texas A&M University, Department of Botany, College Station.

1995   Plant Remains Recovered from Fire-cracked Rock Features Excavated 41VV1697, an Archaic-age Terrace Campsite on the Devil's River. Ms. on file at Center for Ecological Archaeology, Texas A&M University, College Station, Texas, and Amistad National Recreation Area, Del Rio, Texas.

1997   In Search of the Lost Legume: Identifying and Plugging Data Gaps in the Paleodiet of Archaic Period Hunter-Gatherers Living at the Edge of the Southern Plains. Paper presented at the 68th Annual Meeting of the Texas Archeological Society, Midland, Texas, November 2, 1997.

1999   Earth-Oven Plant Processing in Archaic Period Economies: An Example from a Semi-Arid Savannah in South-Central North America. *American Antiquity* 64(4):659-674.

Dering, J. Phil (editor)
1998   *Archaeological Context and Land Use in the Western Rio Grande Plains: Phase II Evaluations at Eleven Sites on the Laughlin Air Force Base, Val Verde County, Texas.* Technical Report No. 1. Center for Ecological Archaeology, Texas A&M University, College Station.

Dibble, David S.
1965   *Bonfire Shelter: A Stratified Bison Kill Site in the Amistad Reservoir Area, Val Verde County, Texas.* Texas Archeological Salvage Project Miscellaneous Papers 3. University of Texas, Austin.

1967   *Excavations at Arenosa Shelter, 1965-1966.* Report submitted to the National Park Service by Texas Archeological Salvage Project. University of Texas, Austin.

1970   On the Significance of Additional Radiocarbon Dates from Bonfire Shelter, Texas. *Plains Anthropologist* 15(50):251-254.

Dibble, David S., and Dessamae Lorrain
1968   *Bonfire Shelter: A Stratified Bison Kill Site, Val Verde County, Texas.* Miscellaneous Papers No. 1. Texas Memorial Museum, The University of Texas at Austin.

Dibble, David S., and Elton R. Prewitt
1967   *Survey and Test Excavations at Amistad Reservoir, 1964-65.* Texas Archeological Salvage Project Survey Reports No. 3. The University of Texas at Austin.

Direccion General De Geografia
1980   *Carta Topografica.* Ciudad Acuna, H14-7, 1:250,000. Coordinacion General de los Servicios Nacionales de Estadistica, Geografia E Informatica. Mexico, D.F.

Ditton Robert B., and David J. Schmidly
1977   *A User Resource Analysis of Amistad Recreation Area.* Texas Agricultural Experiment Station, Texas A&M University, College Station, Texas. Prepared for the Office of Natural Resources, Southwest Region, National Park Service, Santa Fe, New Mexico, Contract No. CX702960169.

Dolman, W. E.

    1995   The Railroad, A Story Line for Seminole Canyon State Historical Park. In *41VV540, a Railroad Era Industrial Site in Seminole Canyon State Historical Park, Val Verde County, Texas*, by Solveig A. Turpin. Texas Parks and Wildlife Department, Cultural Resources Program Publication 95-1. Austin, Texas.

Dymond, Jan Z.

    1976   The Paradox of the Lower Pecos. Unpublished manuscript on file at the Department of Anthropology, The University of Texas at Austin.

Epstein, Jeremiah F.

    1960   *Centipede and Damp Caves: Excavations in Val Verde County, Texas, 1958.* Report submitted to the National Park Service by the Texas Archeological Salvage Project, University of Texas, Austin.

    1969   *The San Isidro Site: An Early Man Campsite in Nuevo Leon, Mexico.* Anthropology Series No. 7. The University of Texas at Austin.

Favata, Martin A., and José B. Fernandez

    1993   *The Account: Álvar Núñez Cabeza de Vaca's Relación.* Arte Público Press, Houston, Texas.

Feder, Kenneth L.

    1997   Site Survey. In *Field Methods in Archeology*, 7th ed., by T.R. Hester, H.J. Shafer, and K.L. Feder, pp 41-68. Mayfield Publishing Company, Mountain View, California.

Fenneman, Nevin M.

    1931   *Physiography of Western United States.* McGraw-Hill Book Company, Inc. New York.

Golden, M.L., W.J. Gabriel, and J.W. Stevens.

    1982   *Soil Survey of Val Verde County, Texas.* U.S. Department of Agriculture. Soil Conservation Service, Washington, D.C.

González Rul, F.

    1990   *Reconocimiento Arqueologico en al parte Mexicana de la Presa de al Amdistad.* Instituto Nacional de Antropologia e Historia, Roma, Mexico.

Graham, John A., and William A. Davis

    1958   *Appraisal of the Archeological Resources of Diablo Reservoir, Val Verde County, Texas.* Report submitted to the National Park Service by the Texas Archeological Salvage Program, The University of Texas at Austin.

Greer, John W.

    1968   *The Cammack Site: A Neo-American Pit-Oven Ring Midden Site in Val Verde County, Texas.* Master's thesis, University of Texas at Austin.

Griffen, W.B.

1969   *Culture Change and Shifting Population in Central Northern Mexico.* Anthropological Papers No. 13. University of Arizona Press, Tucson.

Gustavson, T.C., and M.B. Collins

1998   *Geoarchaeological Investigations of Rio Grande Terrace and Flood Plain Alluvium from Amistad Dam to the Gulf of Mexico.* Technical Series 49. Texas Archaeological Research Laboratory, The University of Texas and Archaeological Studies Program Report No. 12, Texas Department of Transportation, Austin.

Hatch, Stephan L., Kancheepuram N. Gandhi, and Larry E. Brown

1990   *Checklist of the Vascular Plants of Texas.* Texas Agricultural Experiment Station Publication MP-1655. Texas A&M University, College Station.

Hester, Thomas R.

1980   *Digging Into South Texas Prehistory.* Corona Publishing Company, San Antonio.

1983   Late Paleo-Indian Occupations at Baker Cave, Southwestern Texas. *Bulletin of the Texas Archeological Society* 53:101-119.

1989   An Archeological Synthesis. In *From the Gulf to the Rio Grande: Human Adaptation in Central and South, and Lower Pecos Texas,* by T.R. Hester, S.L. Black, D.G. Steele, B.W. Olive, A.A. Fox, K.J. Reinhard, and L.C. Bement, pp. 115-128. Research Series No. 33. Arkansas Archeological Survey, Fayetteville.

1995   The Prehistory of South Texas. *Bulletin of the Texas Archeological Society* 66:427-460.

Heubner, J.

1991   Cactus for Dinner, Again! An Isotopic Analysis of Late Archaic Diet in the Lower Pecos Region of Texas. In *Papers on Lower Pecos Prehistory,* edited by S. Turpin, pp. 175-190. Studies in Archeology Vol. 8. Texas Archeological Research Laboratory, Austin.

Hill, R.T.

1891   Notes on the Geology of the Southwest. *American Geologist* 7:254-255, 336-370.

Hitchcock, R.K., and L.E. Bartram

1998   Social Boundaries, Technical Systems, and the Use of Space and Technology in the Kalahari. In *The Archaeology of Social Boundaries,* edited by M.T. Stark, pp. 12-49. Smithsonian Institution Press, Washington, D.C.

Hoyt, Cathryn A.

2000   Grassland to Desert: Holocene Vegetation and Climatic Change in the Northern Chihuahuan Desert. Ph.D. dissertation, Department of Geography, The University of Texas at Austin.

Hyman, M., and M.W. Rowe

1997   Plasma-Chemical Extraction and AMS Radiocarbon Dating of Pictographs. *American Indian Rock Art* 23:1-9.

Ilger, W. A., M. Hyman, and M. A. Rowe
    1994   Radiocarbon Date for a Red Linear Style Pictograph. *Bulletin of the Texas Archaeological Society* 65: 337-346.

Ilger, W. A., M. Hyman, J. Southon, and M. A. Rowe
    1995   Dating Pictographs with Radiocarbon. *Radiocarbon* 37(2): 299-310.

Irving, R.S.
    1966   The Preliminary Analysis of Plant Remains from Six Amistad Reservoir Sites. In *A Preliminary Study of the Paleoecology of the Amistad Reservoir Area*, edited by D.A. Story and V.M. Bryant, pp. 61-90. The University of Texas at Austin.

Jackson, A.T.
    1938   *Picture Writing of Texas Indians*. University of Texas Publications 3809, Austin.

Johnson, Leroy, Jr.
    1964   *The Devil's Mouth Site: A Stratified Campsite at Amistad Reservoir, Val Verde County, Texas*. Archeology Series No. 6. Department of Anthropology, The University of Texas at Austin.

    1994   *The Life and Times of Toyah-Culture Folk: The Buckhollow Encampment, Site 41KM16, Kimble County, Texas*. Office of the State Archeologist Report 38. Texas Department of Transportation and Texas Historical Commission, Austin.

Kelley, J. Charles, T.N. Campbell, and Donald J. Lehmer
    1940   The Association of Archaeological Materials with Geological Deposits in the Big Bend Region of Texas. *West Texas Historical and Scientific Society Publication 10*. Alpine, Texas.

Kelly, R. L.
    1995   *The Foraging Spectrum*. Smithsonian Institution Press, Washington, D.C.

Kirkland, Forrest, and W.W. Newcomb, Jr.
    1967   *The Rock Art of Texas Indians*. University of Texas Press, Austin.

Kuchler, A.W.
    1964   *Potential Natural Vegetation of the Conterminous United States*. American Geographical Society, New York, NY.

Labadie, Joseph H.
    1994   *Amistad National Recreation Area: A cultural Resource Study*. National Park Service, Santa Fe.

Lord, Kenneth James
    1984   *The Zooarcheology of Hinds Cave, Val Verde County, Texas*. Unpublished Ph.D. dissertation, Department of Anthropology, Texas A&M University, College Station.

Mallouf, Robert

    1987   *Las Haciendas: A Cairn-Burial Assemblage from Northeastern Chihuahua, Mexico.* Office of the State Archeologist Report 35. Texas Historical Commission. Austin, Texas.

Marks, M.K., J.C. Rose, and E.L. Buie

    1988   Bioarchaeology of Seminole Sink. In *Seminole Sink: Excavation of a Vertical Shaft Tomb, Val Verde County, Texas,* compiled by S. Turpin, pp. 75-118. Research Report No. 93. Texas Archeological Survey, The University of Texas at Austin.

Marmaduke, W.S.

    1978   *Prehistoric Culture in Trans-Pecos Texas: An Ecological Approach.* Ph.D. dissertation, Department of Anthropology, The University of Texas at Austin.

Marmaduke, W.S., and Hayden Whitsett

    1975   An Archaeological Reconnaissance in the Devil's River-Dolan Falls Area. In *Devil's River,* edited by Don Kennard, pp. 76-109. Texas Natural Areas Survey No. 4. The University of Texas at Austin.

Martin, George C.

    1933   *Archeological Exploration of the Shumla Caves.* Witte Memorial Museum Bulletin 3, San Antonio.

McClurkan, Burney B.

    1968   *Test Excavations, Javelina Bluff, Val Verde County, Texas.* Report submitted to the National Park Service by the Texas Archeological Salvage Project, The University of Texas at Austin.

McGregor, Roberta

    1992   *Prehistory basketry of the Lower Pecos, Texas.* Monographs in World Archeology 6. Prehistory Press, Madison, Wisconsin.

Mayberry, James D.

    1997   The System-wide Archeological Inventory Program: Amistad National Recreation Area, Val Verde County, Texas. Unpublished manuscript on file with the Anthropology Projects Program, National Park Service, Santa Fe, NM.

Mehalchick, Gemma, and Douglas K. Boyd

    1999   Water in the Desert: Prehistoric Occupations at San Felipe Springs. *In Val Verde on the Sunny Rio Grande: Geoarcheological and Historical Investigations at San Felipe Springs, Val Verde County, Texas,* pp. 149-160. By Gemma Mehalchick, Terri Meyers, Karl W. Kibler, and Douglas K. Boyd. Reports of Investigations Number 122. Prewitt and Associates. Austin, Texas.

Mehalchick, Gemma, Terri Meyers, Karl W. Kibler, and Douglas K. Boyd

    1999   *Val Verde on the Sunny Rio Grande: Geoarcheological and Historical Investigations at San Felipe Springs, Val Verde County, Texas.* Reports of Investigations Number 122. Prewitt and Associates. Austin, Texas.

Nance, Roger C.
    1992   *The Archaeology of La Calsada: A Rockshelter in the Sierra Madre Oriental, Mexico.*
                University of Texas Press, Austin.

North, G.R., George Bomar, John Griffiths, James Norwine, and Juan B. Valdes
    1995   The Changing Climate of Texas. In *The Impact of Global Warming on Texas*, edited by
                G.R. North, Jurgen Schmandt, and J. Clarkson, pp.24-49. University of Texas Press,
                Austin.

Norwine, Jim
    1995   The Regional Climate of South Texas: Patterns and Trends. In *The Changing Climate of*
                Texas, edited by Jim Norwine, J. Giardino, G.R. North, J. Valdes, pp. 138-155.
                GeoBooks, Texas A&M University. College Station, Texas.

Nunley, John P., Lathel F. Duffield, and Edward B. Jelks
    1965   *Excavations at Amistad Reservoir, 1962 Season.* Texas Archeological Salvage Project,
                Miscellaneous Papers No. 3. University of Texas, Austin.

Office of the State Climatologist
    1987   *Climates of Texas Counties.* Graduate School of Business, The University of Texas at
                Austin.

Parsons, Mark L.
    1986   Painted Pebbles: Styles and Chronology. In *Ancient Texans: Rock Art and Lifeways long*
                the Lower Pecos, by Harry Shafer, pp. 180-185. Witte Museum, San Antonio, Texas.

Patton, Peter C., and David S. Dibble
    1982   Archaeologic and Geomorphic Evidence for the Paleohydraulic Record of the Pecos River
                in West Texas. *American Journal of Science* 282:97-121.

Pearce, J.E., and A.T. Jackson
    1933   *A Prehistoric Rock Shelter in Val Verde County, Texas.* Bulletin No. 3324. The
                University of Texas at Austin.

Plog, S., F. Plog, and W. Wait
    1978   Decision making in modern surveys. In *Advances in Archaeological Method and Theory*,
                vol 1, edited by M.B. Schiffer, pp. 383-421. Academic Press, San Diego.

Prewitt, Elton R.
    1966   *A Preliminary Report on the Devil's Rockshelter Site, Val Verde County, Texas.* Texas
                Journal of Science 18(2):206-224.

Raun, Gerald
    1966   A Vertebrate Paleofauna of Amistad Reservoir. In *A Preliminary Study of the*
                Paleoecolofgy of the Amistad Reservoir Area, assembled by D.A. Story and V.M. Bryant,
                pp. 209-220. Final Report of Research under the Auspices of the National Science
                Foundation.

Reinhard, K. J., B.W. Olive, and D.G. Steele
  1989   Bioarcheological Synthesis. In *From the Gulf to the Rio Grande: Human Adaptation in Central, South, and Lower Pecos Texas,* edited by T.R. Hester, S.L. Black, D.G. Steele, B.W. Olive, A.A. Fox, K.J. Reinhard, and L.C. Bement, pp. 129-140. Research Series 33. Arkansas Archeological Survey, Fayetteville.

Russ, Jon, Russell Palma, David Lloyd, Thomas Boutton, and Michael Coy
  1996   Origin of the Whewellite-Rich Rock Crust in the Lower Pecos Region of Southwest Texas and Its Significance to Paleoclimate Reconstructions. *Quaternary Research* 46:27-46.

Sanchez, J.M.
  1999   *Archeological Reconnaissance of Upper Fresno Canyon Rim Big Bend Ranch State Park, Texas.* Reports in Contract Archeology No. 1. Center for Big Bend Studies, Sul Ross State University, Alpine, Texas.

Saunders, Joe W.
  1986   *The Economy of Hinds Cave.* Ph.D. dissertation, Department of Anthropology, Southern Methodist University, Dallas, Texas.

  1992   Plant and Animal Procurement Sites in the Lower Pecos Region, Texas. *Journal of Field Archaeology* 19:335-349.

Schmidt, R.H.
  1986   Chihuahuan Climate. In *Invited Papers from the Second Symposium on Resources of the Chihuahuan Desert Region, U.S. and Mexico*, edited by J.C. Barlow, A.M. Powell, and B.N. Timmermann. CDRI, Alpine, Texas.

  1995   The Climate of Greater Trans-Pecos Texas. In *The Changing Climate of Texas*, edited by Jim Norwine, J. Giardino, G.R. North, J. Valdes, pp. 138-155. GeoBooks, Texas A&M University, College Station.

Schroeder, Albert H., and Dan S. Matson
  1965   *A Colony on the Move: Gaspar Castano de Sosa's Journal, 1590-1591.* The School of American Research, Santa Fe, New Mexico.

Setzler, Frank M.
  1934   Cave Burials in Southwestern Texas. *Explorations and Fieldwork of the Smithsonian Institution in 1933*, pp. 35-37. Washington.

Shafer, Harry J.
  1975   Clay Figurines from the Lower Pecos Region, Texas. *American Antiquity* 40(2):148-158.

  1976   Defining the Archaic: An Example from the Lower Pecos Area of Texas. In *The Texas Archaic: A Symposium*, edited by T.R. Hester, pp. 1-9. Special Report No. 2. Center for Archaeological Research, The University of Texas at San Antonio.

  1981   The Adaptive Technology of the Prehistoric Inhabitants of Southwest Texas. *Plains Anthropologist* 26(92):129-138.

1982   Classic Mimbres Phase Households and Room Use Patterns. *The Kiva* 48(1-2):17-37.

1986   *Ancient Texans: Rock Art and Lifeways Along the Lower Pecos.* Texas Monthly Press, Austin.

1988   The Prehistoric Legacy of the Lower Pecos Region of Texas. *Bulletin of the Texas Archeological Society* 59:23-52. Austin.

1989   The Prehistoric Legacy of the lower Pecos Region of Texas. *Bulletin of the Texas Archeological Society* 59:23-52.

Shafer, Harry J., and Vaughan M. Bryant, Jr.
1977   *Archeological and Botanical Studies at Hinds Cave, Val Verde County, Texas.* Annual Report to the National Science Foundation by the Department of Anthropology, Texas A&M University, College Station.

Simms, S.
1987   *Behavioral Ecology and Hunter-Gatherer Foraging: An Example from the Great Basin.* BAR International Series 381. British Archeological Reports, Oxford.

Skiles, J.
1996   *Judge Roy Bean Country.* Texas Tech University Press. Lubbock, Texas.

Smith, Charles Isaac
1970   *Lower Cretaceous Stratigraphy, Northern Coahuila, Mexico.* Report of Investigations No. 65. Bureau of Economic Geology, Austin, Texas.

Sobolik, K.D.
1991   *Paleonutrition of the Lower Pecos Region of the Chihuahuan Desert.* Ph.D. dissertation, Department of Anthropology, Texas A&M University, College Station.

1996   Nutritional Constraints and Mobility Patterns of Hunter-Gathers in the Northern Chihuahuan Desert. In *Case Studies in Environmental Archeology*, edited by E.J. Reitz, L. A. Newsom, and S.J. Scudder, pp. 195-214. Plenum Press, New York.

Sorrow, William M.
1968   *The Devil's Mouth Site: The Third Season-1967.* Papers of the Texas Archeological Salvage Project No. 14. University of Texas, Austin.

Taylor, Walter W.
1958   Archeological Survey of the Mexican Part of Diablo Reservoir. In *Appraisal of the Archeological Resources of Diablo Reservoir, Val Verde County, Texas.* Mimeographed report prepared by Archeological Salvage Program Field Office, National Park Service, Austin.

1964   Tethered Nomadism and Water Territoriality: An Hypothesis. *Actas Y Memorias del XXXV Congreso Internacional de Americanistas* 1962: 197-203.

Taylor, W.W., and F.G. Rul

    1961   An Archeological Reconnaissance Behind the Diablo Dam, Coahuila, Mexico. *Bulletin of the Texas Archeological Society* 31:153-165.

Thomas, David Hurst

    1983   *The Archeology of Monitor Valley: 2. Gatecliff Shelter.* Anthropological Papers 59, Pt. 1. American Museum of Natural History, New York.

    1988   *The Archeology of Monitor Valley: 3. Survey and Additional Excavations.* Anthropological Papers of the American history Musuem of Natural History, New York.

Thomas, Sidney Johnson

    1933   *The Archeological Investigation of Fate Bell Shelter, Seminole Canyon, Val Verde County, Texas.* Master's thesis, University of Texas at Austin.

Thoms, Alston V.

    1988   A Survey of Predictive Locational Models: Examples from the Late 1970s and Early 1980. In *Quantifying the Present and Predicting the Past: Theory, Method, and Application of Archaeological Predictive Modeling,* edited by W. James Judge and Lynne Sebastian, pp. 581-645. U.S. Department of the Interior, Bureau of Land Management Service Center. Denver, Colorado.

    1992   Late Pleistocene and Early Holocene Regional Land Use Patterns: A Perspective from the Preliminary Results of Archeological Studies at the Richard Beene Sties, 41BX831, Lower Medina River, South Texas. In *Guidebook, 10th Annual Meeting, South-Central Friends of the Pleistocene: Late Cenozoic Alluvial Stratigraphy and Prehistory of the Inner Gulf Coastal Plain, South-Central Texas.* Quaternary Research Center Series 4 (draft). Lubbock Lake Landmark, Texas Tech University, Lubbock.

    1997a   Long-Term Trends in the Use of Rock Heating Elements: Implications for Land-Use Change. Paper presented at the 62nd Annual meeting of the Society for American Archaeology, Nashville, Tennessee.

    1997b   Sacred Guardians, Profane Practitioners and Texans Without History. *Bulletin of the Texas Archaeological Society* 68:191-213.

Turner, Ellen S., and Thomas R. Hester

    1999   *A Field Guide to Stone Artifacts of Texas Indians.* Gulf Publishing, Houston, Texas.

Turpin, Solveig A.

    1982   *Seminole Canyon: The Art and Archeology.* Texas Archeological Survey Research Report 83. The University of Texas at Austin.

    1984   The Red Linear Style Pictographs of the Lower Pecos River Region, Texas. *Plains Anthropologist* 29(105):181-198.

1986   Toward a Definition of a Pictograph Style: The Lower Pecos Bold Line Geometrics. *Plains Anthropologist* 31 (112): 153-161.

1990   Rock Art and Its Contribution to Hunter Gatherer Archaeology: A Case Study from the Lower Pecos River Region of Southwest Texas and Northern Mexico. *Journal of Field Archaeology* 17(3):263-281.

1991   Time out of Mind: The Radiocarbon Chronology of the Lower Pecos River Region. In *Papers on Lower Pecos Prehistory*, edited by S.A. Turpin, pp. 1-49. Studies in Archeology No. 8. Texas Archeological Research Laboratory, The University of Texas at Austin.

1994   On a Wing and a Prayer: Flight Metaphors in Pecos River Pictographs. In *Shamanism and Rock Art in North America,* edited by S.A. Turpin, pp. 73-102. Special Publication No. 1. Rock Art Foundation, Inc., San Antonio, Texas.

1995   Lower Pecos River Region of Texas and Northern Mexico. *Bulletin of the Texas Archeological Society* 66:541-560.

Turpin, S. A. (Compiler)
1988   *Seminole Sink: Excavations of a Vertical Shaft Tomb, Val Verde County, Texas.* Memoir No. 22. Plains Anthropologist 33(122), Part 2.

Turpin, S.A., and J. Bass
1997   *The Lewis Canyon Petroglyphs.* Special Report 2. Rock Art Foundation, Inc. San Antonio, Texas.

Turpin, S.A., and L.C. Bement
1989   The Live Oak Hole Complex: Plains Indian Art and Occupation in the Lower Pecos River Region. *Bulletin of the Texas Archeological Society* 59:65-82.

Turpin, S.A., and M. Davis
1993   The Devils River State Natural Area: The 1989 TAS Field School. *Bulletin of the Texas Archeological Society* 61:1-50.

Van Devender, Thomas R.
1990   Late Quaternary Vegetation and Climate of the Chihuahuan Desert, United States and Mexico. In *Packrat Middens: The Last 40,000 Years of Biotic Change,* edited by J.L. Betancourt, T.R. Van Devender, and P.S.. Martin, pp. 105-133. The University of Arizona Press, Tucson.

Williams-Dean, Glenna
1978   *Ethnobotany and Cultural Ecology of Prehistoric Man in Southwest Texas.* Ph.D. dissertation, Texas A&M University, College Station.

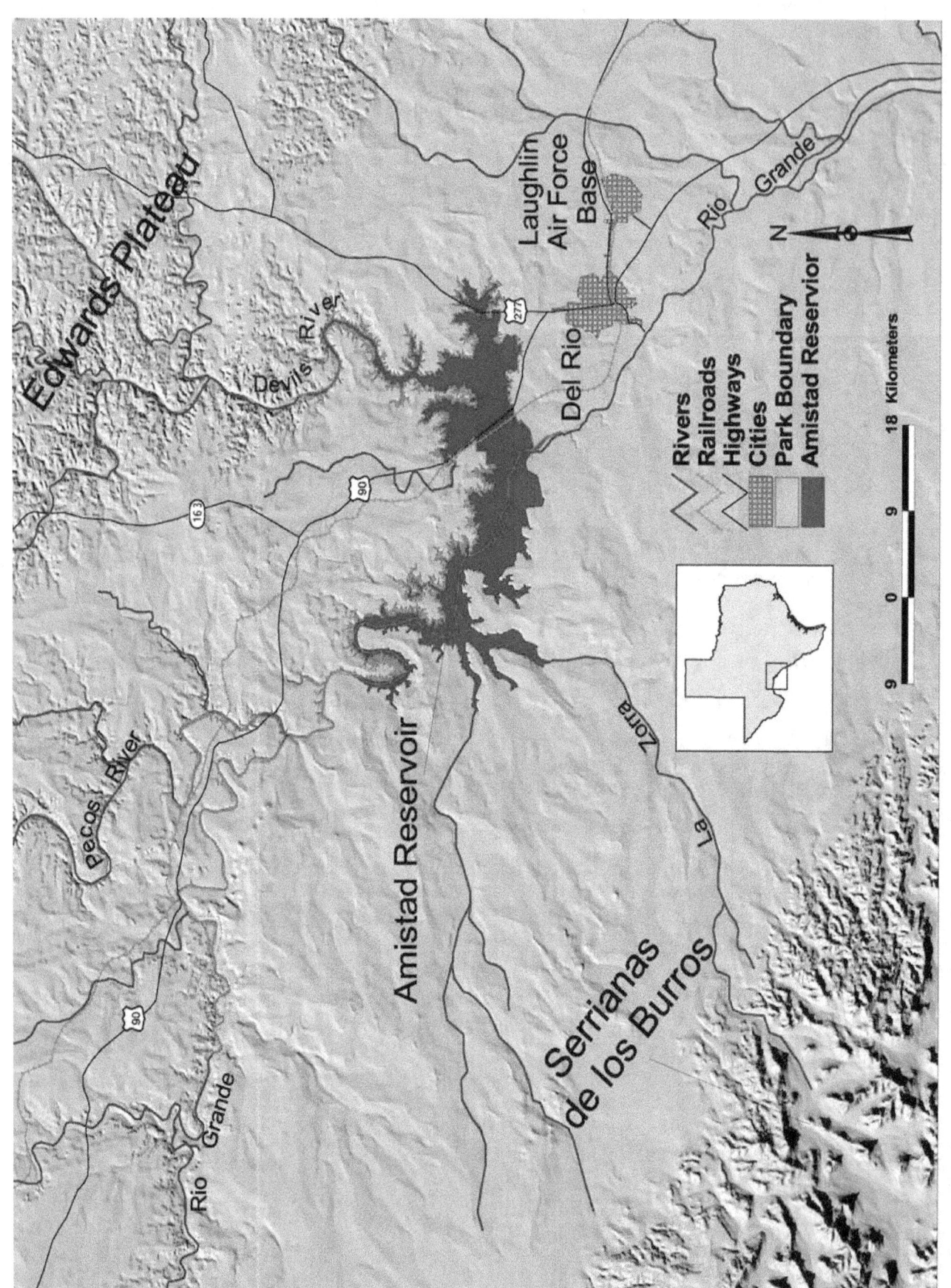

Figure 2.1. Boundary of Amistad National Recreation Area with major drainages and prominent landmarks.

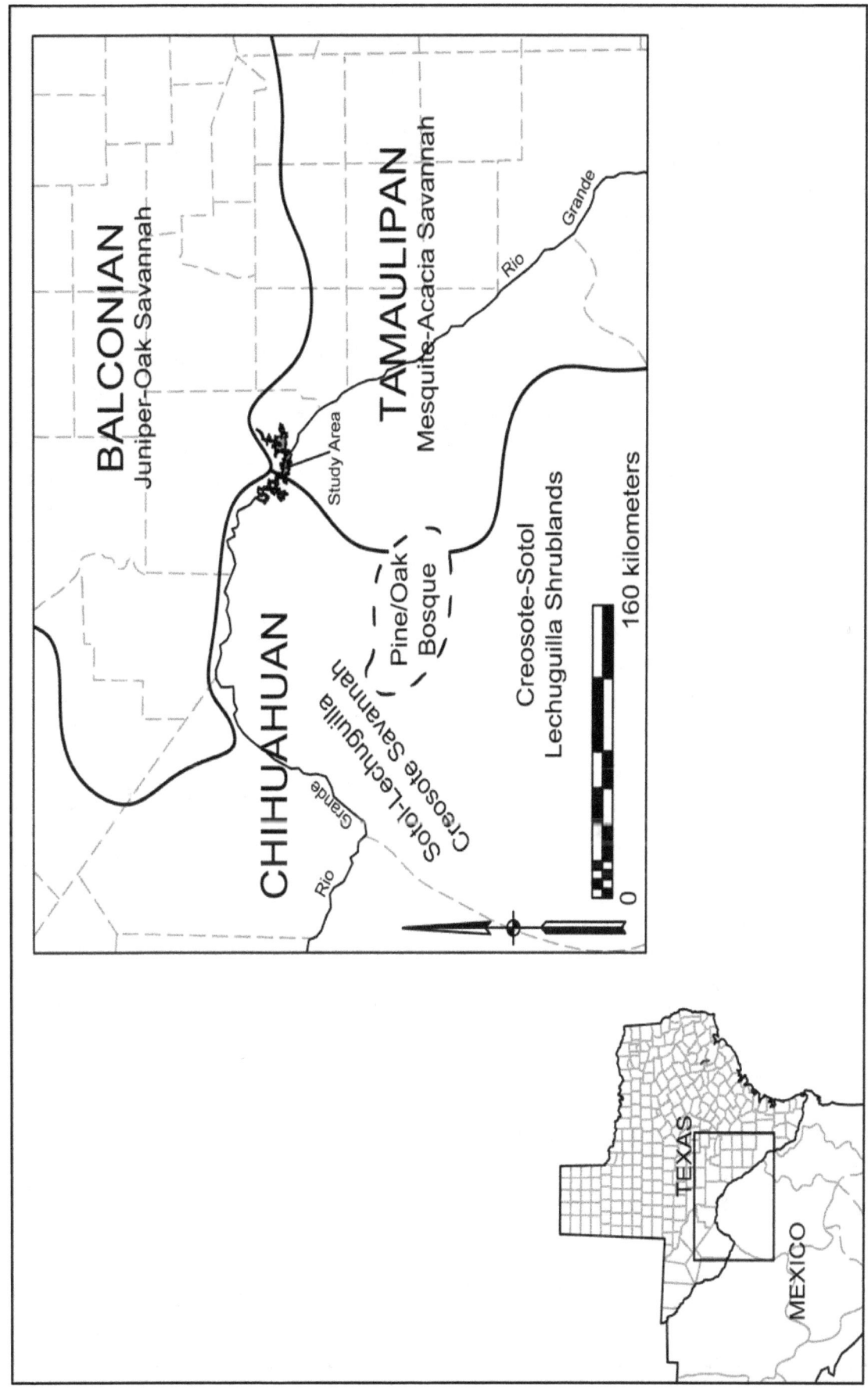

Figure 2.2. Biotic provinces and vegetation types in the study area.

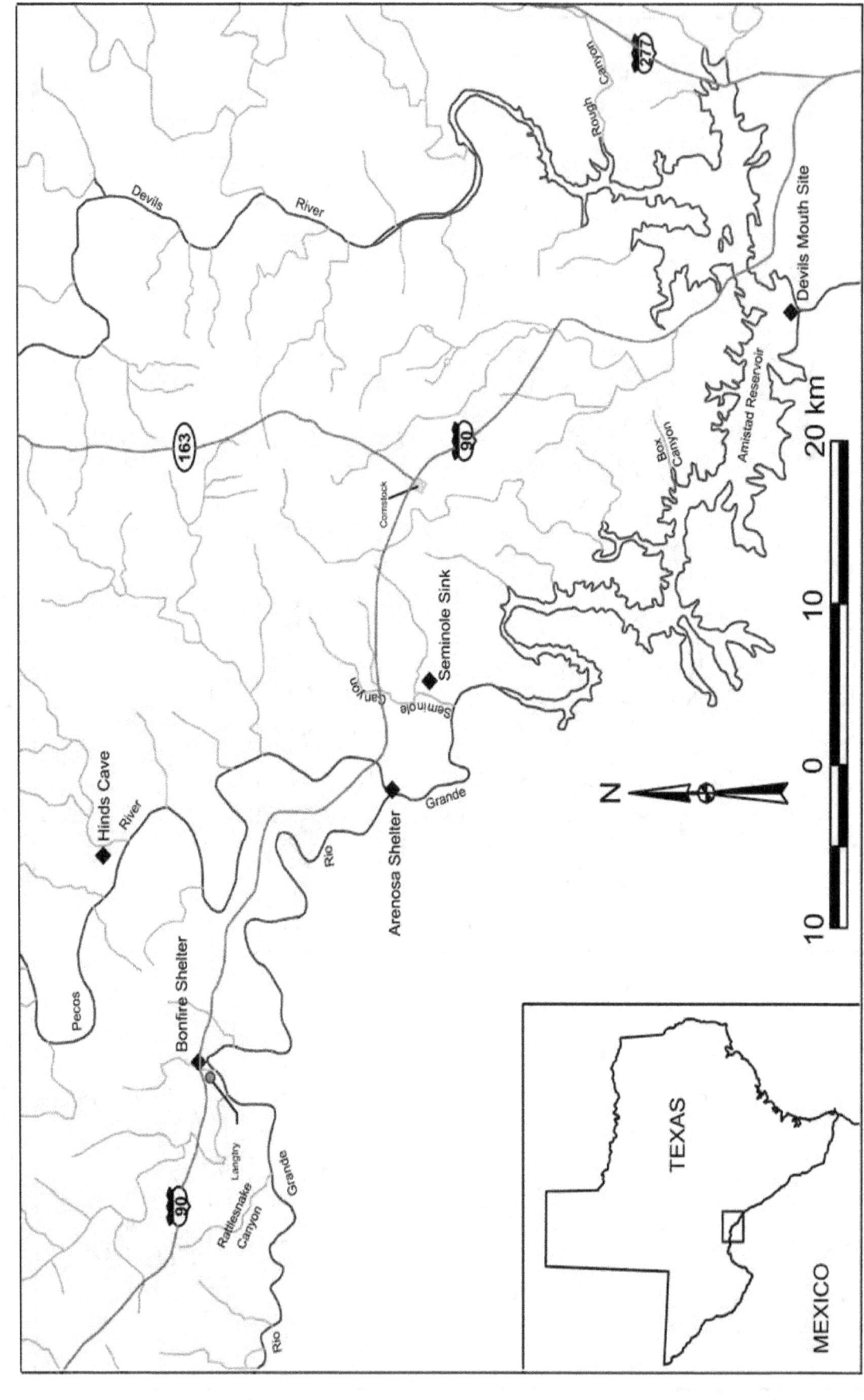

Figure 2.3. Locations of environmental and archeological studies near the Amistad National Recreation Area.

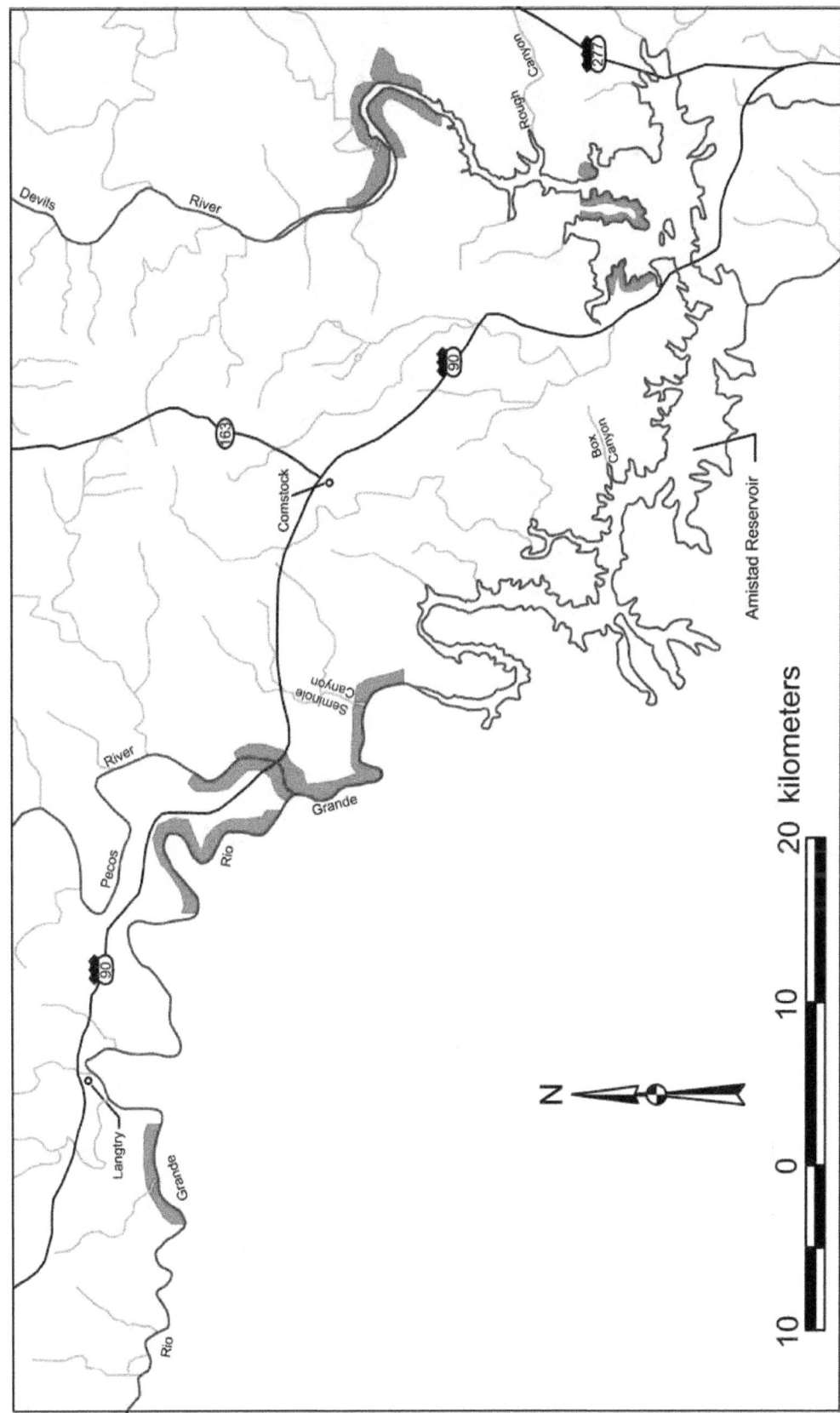

Figure 5.1. Areas surveyed by the Systemwide Archeological Inventory Project, 1992-1993.

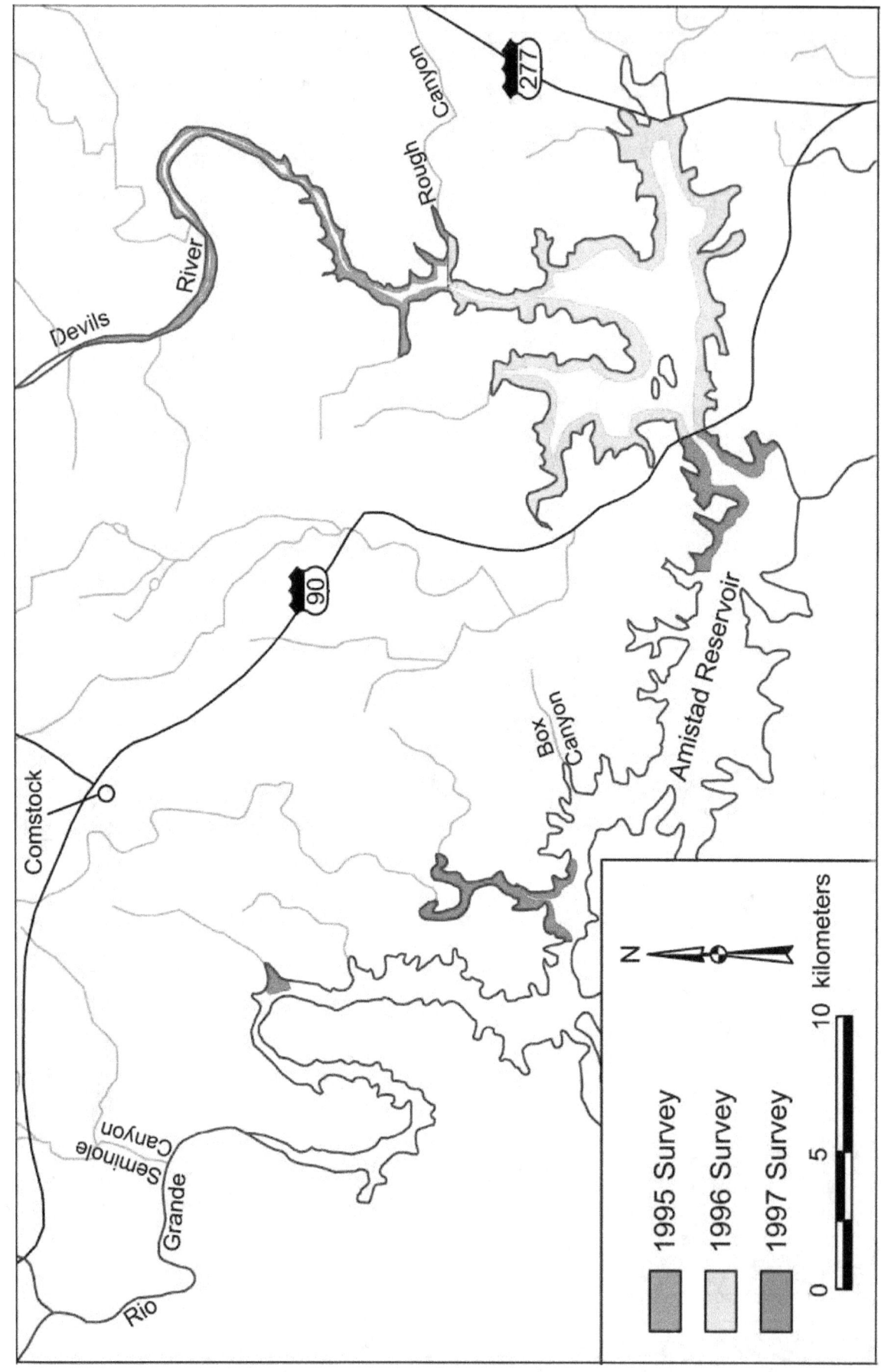

Figure 5.2. Areas surveyed by the low-water surveys of 1995, 1996, and 1997.

Figure 6.1.   Midden deposit in 41 VV 1380.

Figure 6.2. Mortars in boulder resting on surface of midden deposit in 41VV1380.

Figure 6.3. Pestle from 41VV1380.

Figure 6.4. Bold line Geometric style in context of Pecos River style pictographs, Parida Cave (41VV187).

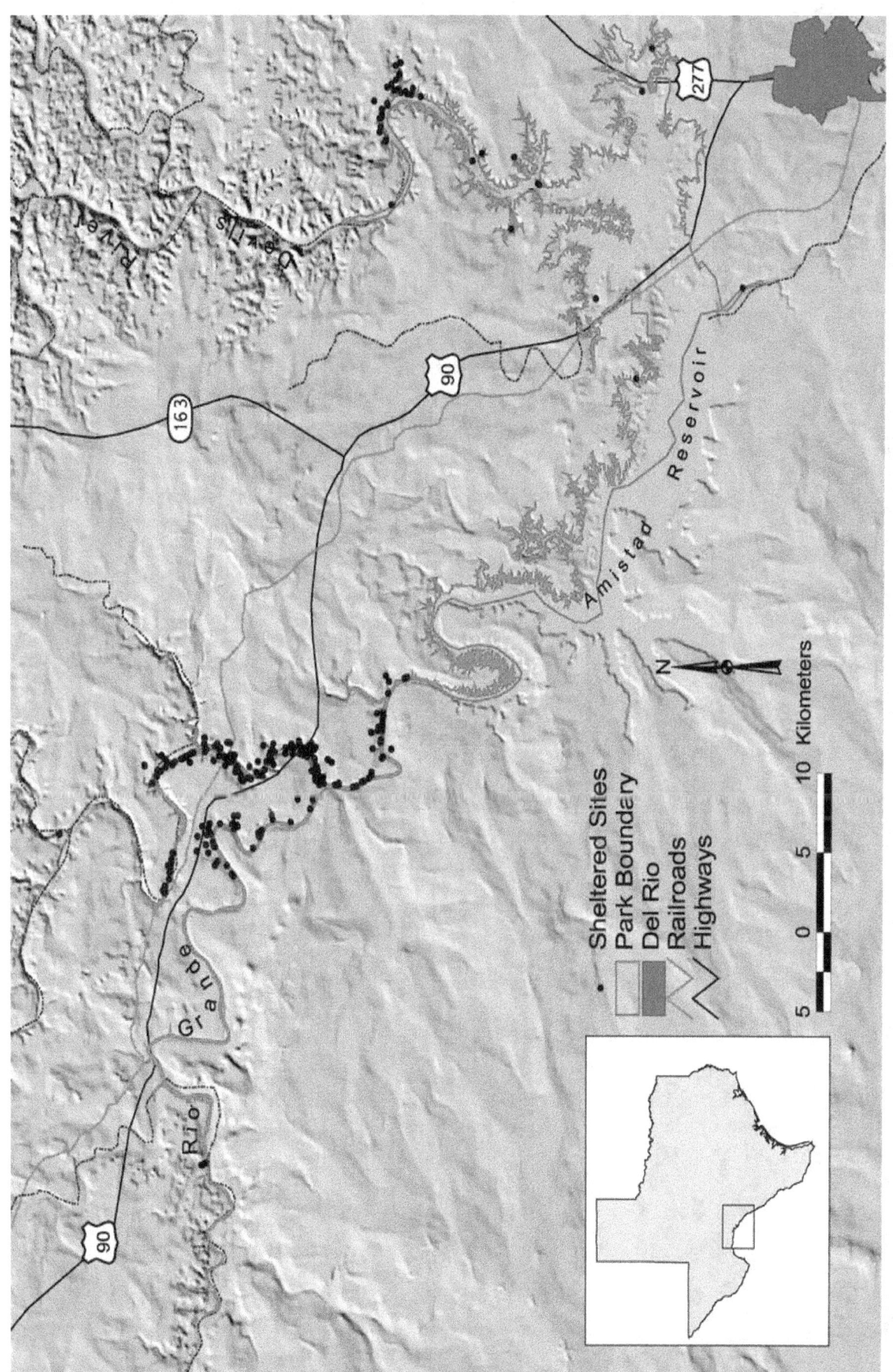

Figure 6.5. Distribution of sheltered sites (caves, overhangs, and rockshelters) within the project area.

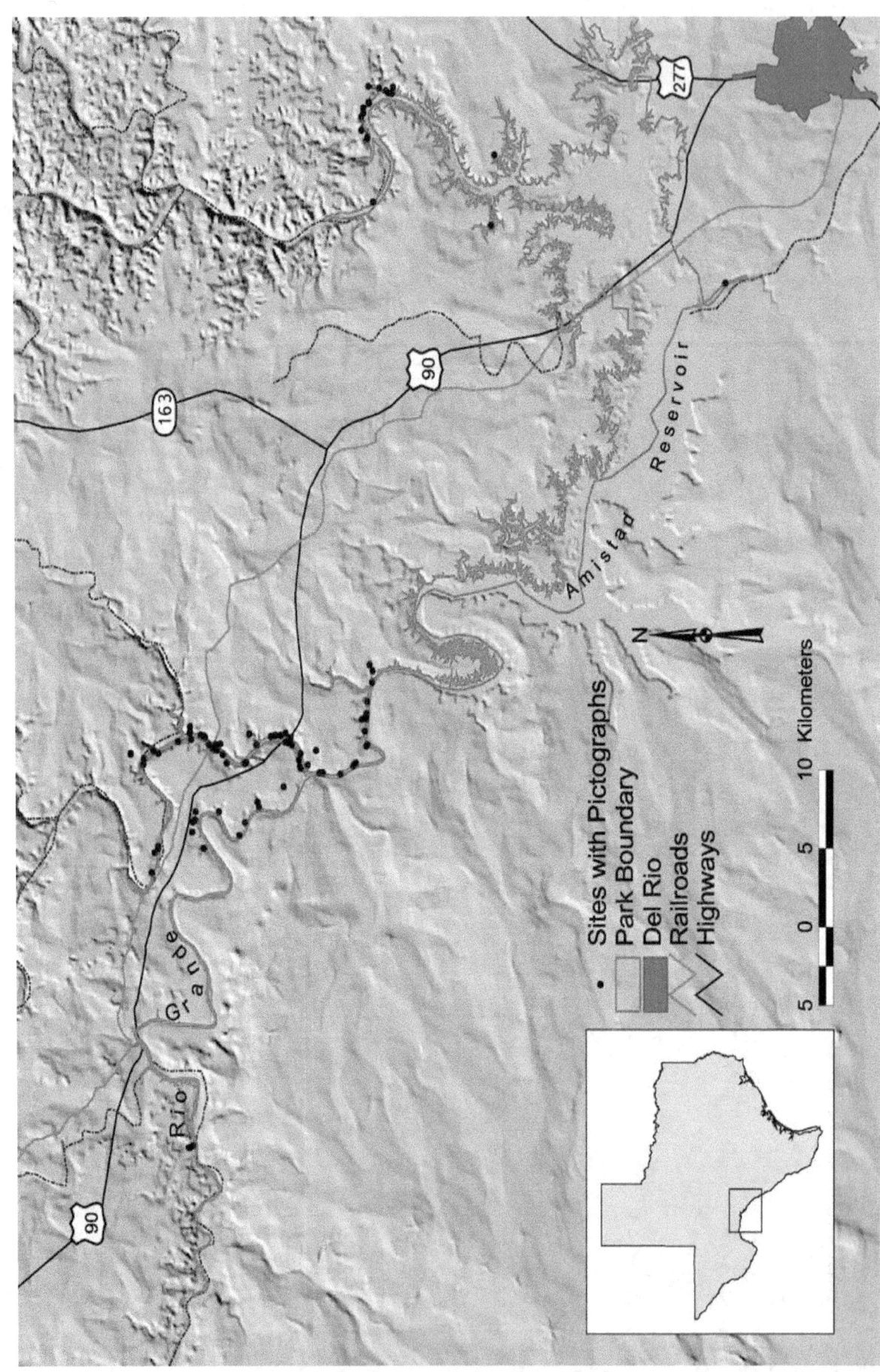

Figure 6.6. Distribution of pictographs within the project area.

Figure 6.7. Site 41VV1694, burned rock midden on terrace of Devils River.

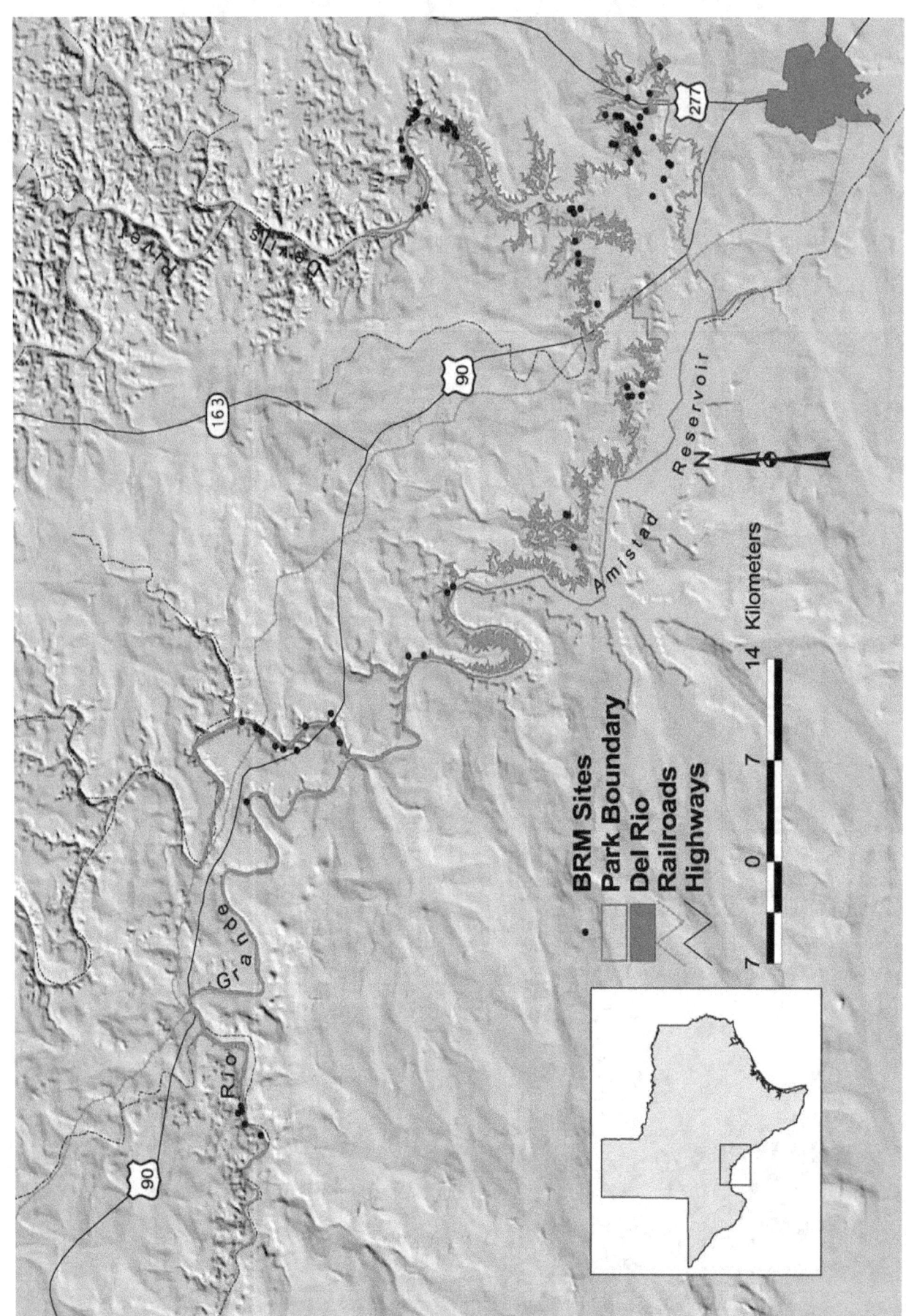

Figure 6.8. Distribution of burned rock midden sites within the project area.

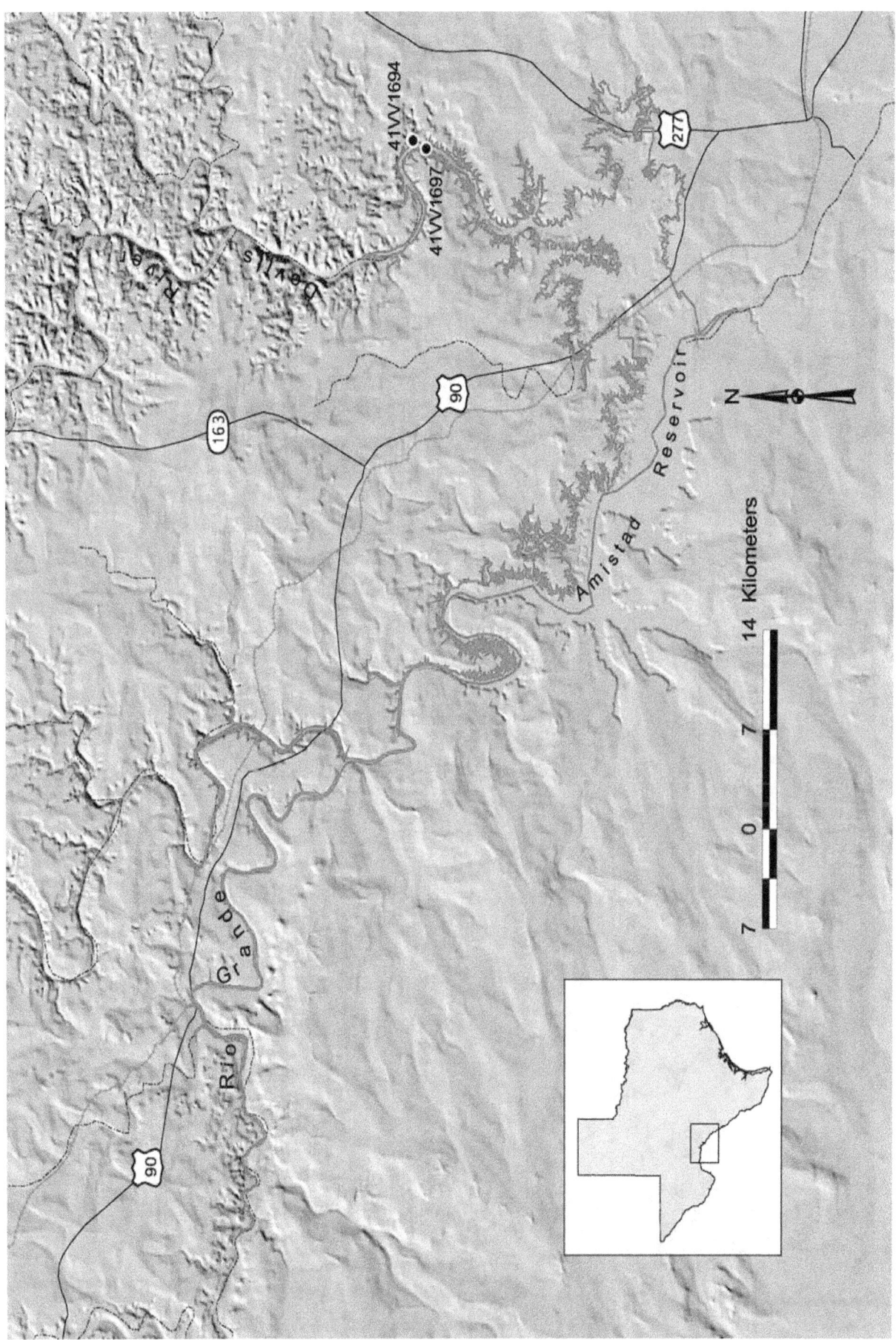

Figure 6.9. Location of 41VV1697, multiple hearths, and 41VV1694, burned rock midden.

Figure 6.10. Hearth, Feature 24, at 41VV1697, a site containing multiple hearths on the western terrace of the Devils River.

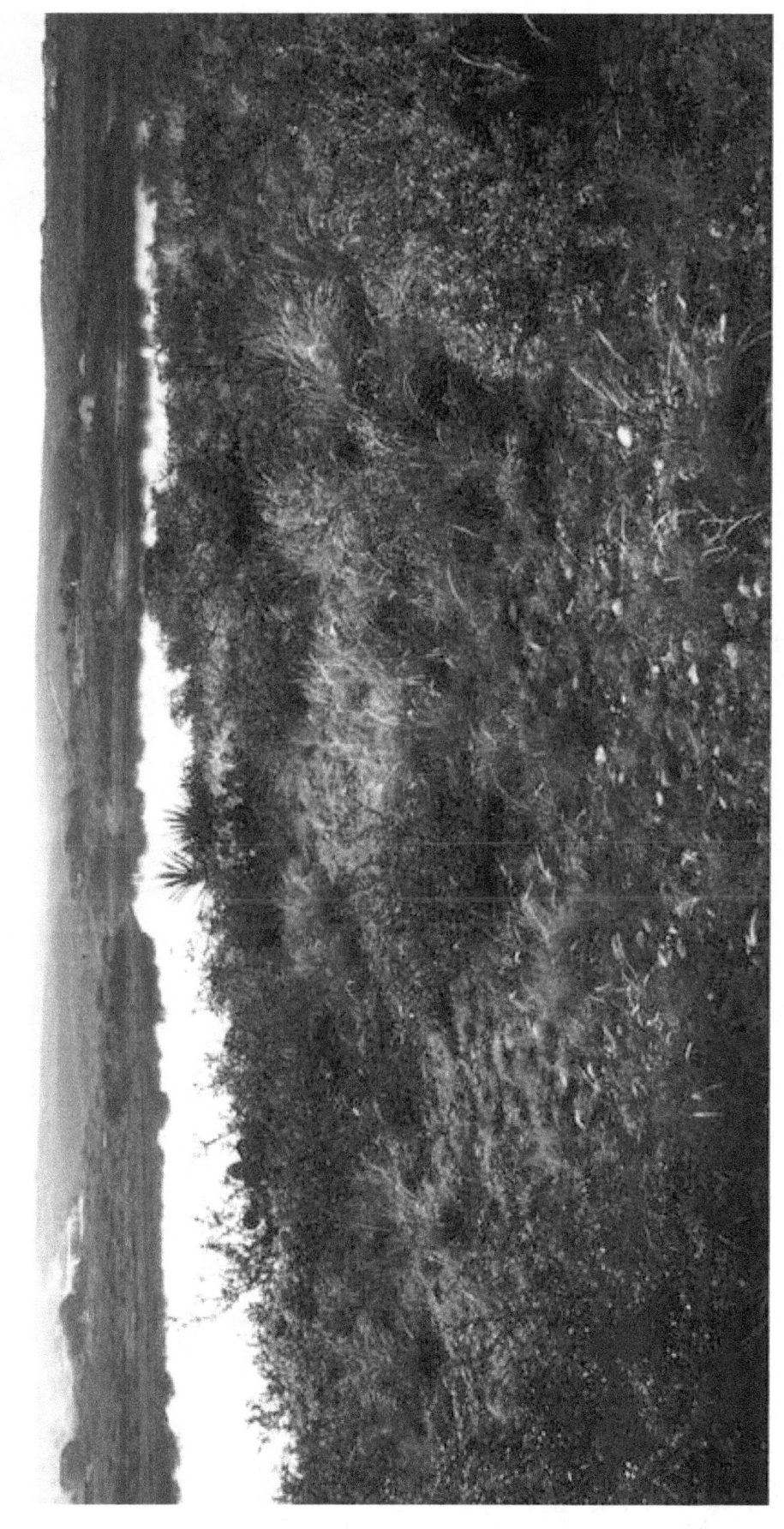

Figure 6.11. Site 41VV1485. a quarry site overlooking the Devils River.

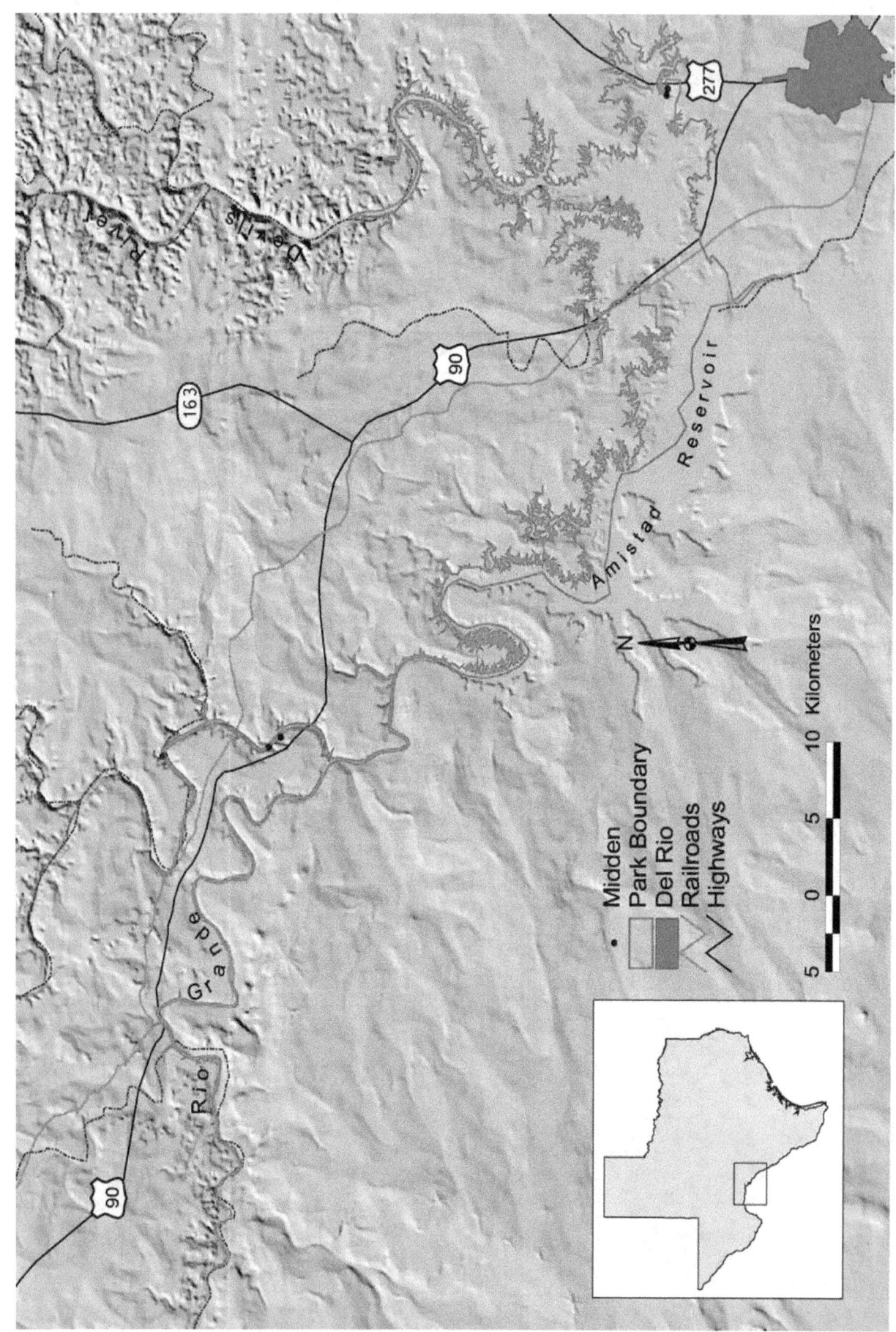

Figure 6.12. Distribution of midden sites within the project area.

Figure 6.13. Lt. Bullis' Trail (41VV1428), view from the Pecos River.